Walking Law and History: Genesis

by Michelle Janene

Sacramento

Note:
The fact that materials produced by other publishers may be referred to in this volume does not constitute an endorsement of the content or theological position of materials produced by such publishers. Any references and ancillary materials are listed as an aid to the student or the teacher and in an attempt to maintain the accepted academic standards of the publishing industry.

Walking the Law and History: Genesis
Walking His Footsteps
First Edition

Author
    Michelle Janene

Editor
    Stephen Mathieson

Cover Design
    D's Concepts and Designs

Cover Photo
    Viorel Sima/Shutterstock

Cover Fonts
    www.kevinandamanda.com
    Simplicity font

Strong Tower Press grants the original purchaser a limited license to copy the reproducible pages contained within this book for use in their classroom. Further reproduction or distribution shall be a violation of this license. Copies may not be sold. Unless otherwise noted, all Scripture quotations are from the New International Version (NIV).

© 2016 Strong Tower Press
Sacramento, California 95828

Printed in the United States
All rights reserved
ISBN: 978-1-942320-04-3

Unit 1 Overview	5
Lesson 1 Creation	6
Lesson 3 Broken Relationships	9
Unit 1 Homework Review 1	13
Lesson 4 First Murder	15
Lesson 5 Too Much Sin	17
Lesson 6 New Beginning	19
Lesson 7 Babbling at the Tower	21
Unit 1 Homework Review 2	23
Unit 1 Verses	25
Unit 2 Overview	27
Lesson 1 Call of Abraham	28
Lesson 2 On Again / Off Again Faith	30
Lesson 3 God's Covenant	32
Lesson 4 Here Let Me Help	33
Unit 2 Homework Review 1	35
Lesson 5 City Lost	37
Lesson 6 Really? A Son at My Age?	39
Lesson 7 The Ultimate Test	41
Lesson 8 The Promise Passes	43
Unit 2 Homework Review 2	49
Lesson 9 Squabbling Twins	51
Lesson 10 Finding a New Home and Purpose	54
Lesson 11 Jacob's Many Blessings	58
Unit 2 Homework 3 (1)	63
Unit 2 Homework 3 (2)	64
Lesson 12 Wrangling Wages	65
Lesson 13 Home Coming	67
Lesson 14 Dream a Little Dream	74
Lesson 15 God's Bumpy Road	77
Unit 2 Homework Review 4	85

Lesson 16 Testing and Changed Hearts 87
Lesson 17 Family Reunion 95
Lesson 18 Foreigners in a Foreign Land 99
Lesson 19 Blessings and Farewells 101
Unit 2 Homework Review 5 105
Unit 2 Verses 107

Unit 1 The Story Begins

Objectives
Students will be able to:
- List the days of creation in order
- Describe the importance of a personal and close relationship with our Creator
- List our responsibilities for the earth
- Memorize key passages
- Describe God's plan for a restored relationship
- Describe God's judgment, forgiveness, and care, for the people in Gen. 1-11

Unit Summary

Lesson One (2)	Creation	Gen. 1-2
Active Lesson	Illustrate Days of Creation	
Lesson Two (2)	How Big is God?	CD presentation
Lesson Three	Broken Relationships	Gen. 3
Review 1-1		
Lesson Four	First Murder	Gen. 4
Lesson Five (2)	Too Much Sin=Too Much Water	Gen. 6-8
Lesson Six	New Beginning – Same Old Sin	Gen 9
Lesson Seven	Babbling at the Tower	Gen. 11:1-9
Review 1-2		

Memory Verses Ps. 119:11, Ps. 9:1-2, Ps. 105:1-3, Jer. 29:11

Unit 1 The Story Begins
Lesson 1 Creation
Gen. 1-2

Essential Question: What things can we learn about God's character from the way He created the universe?

Genesis means 1. _____ and the theme is 2. _____.

Ch. 1-11 is the origins of the 3. _____ _____, and covers about 4. _____ years.

Ch 12-50 is the origins of the 5. _____ _____, and covers about 6. ____ years.

1:1-5 Day 1 God 7. _____, and it was. Is there any object you can create with just your words? God is 8. _____; all-powerful. He speaks and things change, radically.

Notice God created 9. _____ but no 10. _____.

v.6-8 Day 2 God separated the 11. _____ above from the water on the surface of the earth. It would be like a giant greenhouse, warm weather all around the globe, no 12. _____ and no 13. _____.

v. 9-13 Day 3 God 14. _____ the water on the surface so 15. _____ _____ formed, and created 16. _____ to grow on the land. The plants were not seeds God put in the ground, but 17. _____-_____ plants ready to seed and bear fruit.

v. 14-19 Day 4 Now we have the 18. _____, 19. _____, and 20. _____. And with them we have a 21. _____.

v. 20-23 Day 5 God created 22. _____ _____ and 23. _____.

v. 24-26 Day 6 More animals, both 24. _____ and 25. _____.
Then God created the 26. _____ of His creation. Adam was also created as a
27. _____ _____, not a baby.

v. 27-31 Now God created with His 28. _____. We are made in 29. _____
_____. This doesn't mean that we look like God, but we are 30. _____
and possess the 31. _____ of God.
The first thing God did was 32. _____ humans. We were meant to 33. _____
the earth and the things in and on it, but we were not to 34. _____ and destroy it.
Notice that at this time v.29-30 all creatures are 35. _____.
Each day God looked at what He had done and said it was 36. _____. But after
creating us He said it was 37. _____ _____.

2:1-3 Day 7 God 38. _____. God made us a structure of 39. _____
(40. ____-day weeks), and showed us an example of the 41. _____ we would
receive when we followed Him and rested.

v. 4-14 Verse 4 is the first time 42. _____ is used. The name God called Himself.

The word "formed" in v. 7 יצר *yatsar* describes the work of an 43. _____. You are
God's 44. _____.
God breathed life into man. The word for breath is the same word for Spirit. God put His
45. _____, His 46. _____ in man.

v. 15-25 God took Adam (name means 47. _____ ____ _____) and placed
him in the garden to "48. _____ it and take care of it" and name the animals. Work is
not a 49. _____ for sin.
This is a truth we will see again and again in the Old Testament. It is the main theme of the

Bible:

50. _____ = 51. _____ /

52. _____ = 53. _____ .

Therefore, Eve was created from Adam's 54. _____ to help carry his 55. _____. She was designed to 56. _____ him.

Helping is not 57. _____. 58. _____ is most important in God's sight.

Now, at first Adam and Eve were 59. _____. There are 2 different thoughts on why they were not 60. _____.

Assignment: Use **anything** you want and create a model, diagram, illustration, or representation of the days of creation. Extra points will be given for creativity.

Unit 1 The Story Begins
Lesson 3 Broken Relationships
Genesis 3

Essential Question: How did the first sin effect relationships?

v. 1-7 "The Word of the Lord brought 1. _____ and 2. _____; the word of the serpent brought 3. _____ and 4. _____."

Satan came in the form of a serpent, reminding us that temptation comes in 5. _____.

† How is your personal Bible study going? _____
_____

Eve's mistake was 6. _____ the matter with Satan. Satan also attacked God's 7. _____, saying that God was keeping something from Eve.

Wisdom is never attained by 8. _____ God's Word." According to Prov. 1:7 where does real wisdom come from? 9. _____

First Adam and Eve noticed they were 10. _____.

v. 8-13 Adam and Eve did not drop dead on the spot, but their bodies did start to 11. _____ and die at that moment, and they died 12. _____.

Next they 13. _____ from God. God came every night and 14. _____ with Adam and Eve.

God is 15. _____: all knowing.

But, true of sin, with the first sin came the first 16 _____.

First, Adam pointed the finger at 17. _____ for his own disobedience. Next he pointed the finger at 18. _____.

Sin is 19. _____, and God deals with each of us 20. _____. Not as a group or even a pair. But Eve followed her husband's 21. _____ and pointed her finger at the serpent.

v. 14-15 "You will crawl on your 22. _____." 'I will put 23. _____ between serpents and people.'

God told Adam and Eve one day a 24. _____ of theirs would come Who would take Satan out. Satan just learned his days were 25. _____.

v. 16 Next God turned to Eve. Women would now have *increased* 26. _____ in having children. The 27. _____ was broken between them.

v. 17-19 Now to Adam. Adam didn't just sin, he 28. _____ his 29. _____ over 30. _____. Where work was designed 31. _____ the fall, it was a 32. _____. Now work would be 33. _____ _____, 34. _____, and yield 35. _____ _____.

The punishment of death is actually part of God's 36. _____. These punishments were 37. _____.

People will die and 38. _____ _____ _____ in the chaotic painful state, 39. _____ will be born to continue the human race, and 40. _____ _____ will come from one of their great, great, great… grandchildren.

Consequences of the first sin:

Before	**After**
Life	41. _____
Pleasure	42. _____
Abundance	43. _____
Perfect Fellowship	44. _____

v. 20 Adam 45. _____ God's promise for children.

v. 21-24 Adam and Eve now saw the horrible 46. _____ for their sin. The first death in all of history was an 47. _____ life. There is no 48. _____ without 49. _____. 50. _____ blood provides the perfect payment for our sins—the final blood offering.

Cherubim are always linked to 51. _____ _____ and associated with entering into God's 52. _____. Their image was used as decorations all over the 53. _____.

Name _____

Unit 1 Homework Review #1

1. List the days of creation in order.

   1. _____   2. _____

   3. _____   4. _____

   5. _____   6. _____

2. What did God do on the seventh day? _____

3. How did God create the world? _____

4. How did God create people? _____

5. Read Gen. 1:27 and 3:8-9 What was God's relationship with people like before the fall?
   _____

6. What does it mean when people say, "Showing disrespect to others is showing disrespect to God"? _____

7. What task(s) did God give Adam? 2:15, 19-20 _____
   _____

8. Why did God create woman? 2:18 and 1:28 _____

9. What did God do to cover Adam and Eve? _____

10. How did God show mercy to Adam and Eve? _____
    _____

Name _____

Unit 1 Homework Review #1

1. List the days of creation in order.

   1. _____   2. _____
   3. _____   4. _____
   5. _____   6. _____

2. What did God do on the seventh day? _____

3. How did God create the world? _____

4. How did God create people? _____

5. Read Gen. 1:27 and 3:8-9 What was God's relationship with people like before the fall?
   _____

6. What does it mean when people say, "Showing disrespect to others is showing disrespect to God"? _____

7. What task(s) did God give Adam? 2:15, 19-20 _____
   _____

8. Why did God create woman? 2:18 and 1:28 _____

9. What did God do to cover Adam and Eve? _____

10. How did God show mercy to Adam and Eve? _____
    _____

Unit 1 The Story Begins
Lesson 4 First Murder
Genesis 4

Essential Question: How does God reveal His mercy in the life of Cain?

v. 1-7 Adam and Eve's first born was 1. _____ (I've got him).

We see 2. _____ and the 3. _____ of animals were practiced. Adam and his descendants did not spend tens of thousands of years living in caves as 4. _____-_____.

Abel brought the best of his 5. _____, and Cain brought some of his 6. _____. Most believe Cain's offering was unacceptable because it was not a 7. _____ sacrifice.

- ❖ A sacrifice is _____

- ❖ An offering is _____

Regardless, the crucial difference was Abel brought his 8. _____, and Cain brought 9. _____. We get the feeling Cain had an attitude of 10. '_____.

Cain could choose to 11. _____ sin and find blessing, or he could 12. _____ _____ to sin and be devoured.

Being righteous is 13. _____ _____. While his mother, Eve, had to be talked 14. _____ sinning, Cain couldn't be talked 15. _____ __ sinning.

At this time, they used one lamb for each 16. _____. Later, at the Passover, they killed one lamb for a 17. _____. Then, at the Day of Atonement, they sacrificed one lamb for the sins of the entire 18. _____. Finally, with Jesus, one Lamb sacrificed Himself to take a the sin of the 19. _____ _____.

v. 8-12 Cain did not want to 20. _____ his ways, so he got rid of his 21. _____. Cain 22. _____ this act.
God questioned Cain with the desire for him to 23. _____.

† Are you a good brother/sister's keeper? Describe one time when you helped or stuck up for someone else. _____

v. 13-16 Cain didn't regret the 24. _____, just the 25. _____.

v. 17-24 Cain must have married a 26. _____ for there were no other women around.

The generations that followed Cain and his son quickly made advancements, like 27. _____ a city, 28. _____ _____, 29. _____, the 30. _____, and 31. _____.

Lamech was the first man recorded to take 32. ___ _____ Lamech was so far from God, he not only didn't try to hide the 33. _____ he committed, but he 34. _____ about it.

v. 25-26 Adam and Eve had 35. _____ unnamed children, but 36. _____ is named because he *replaced* Abel. This is the side of the family that the 37. _____ would come from.

Unit 1 The Story Begins
Lesson 5 Too Much Sin = Too Much Water
Genesis 6-8

Essential Question: How do we understand that God is both a God of love and a God of justice?

v. 1-8 God did not allow the human race to stay in this rebellious place 1. _____.

It may be the number of years between the announcement and when the 2. _____ _____ _____. Or it could be the 3. _____ _____ of humans.

4. _____ *inclination of the* 5. _____ *of his* 6. _____ *was only* 7. _____ *all the time.*

Our 8. _____ of God, hurt His 9. _____.

Noah didn't 10. _____ grace; he 11. _____ it.

v. 9-22 In the midst of such 12. _____ and 13. _____, there is also 14. _____.

15. _____ and _____ make up what the Bible refers to as 16. _____.

Best estimates say there where about 17. _____ different 'Kinds' of animals on the ark.

18. _____ wouldn't have needed to be on the ark because they breath through their skin. With these figures the ark could have held 19. _____ sheep. There were probably about 20. _____ types of dinosaurs on the ark. But 21. _____% of all dinosaur bones are from the flood.

Noah didn't 22. _____, make 23. _____, or 24. _____. He simply 25. _____ what God called him to do.

The Bible presents Noah as a great 26. _____ of God. He was an outstanding 27. _____ of righteousness, a 28. _____ of righteousness.

Ch 7 v. 1-5 Noah spent the years before the flood 29. _____ _____.

Walking Law and History: Genesis/ 18

Noah not only took in 30. _____ of every unclean kind of animal, he was also supposed to take 31. ____ _____ of clean animals.

God can easily get the 32. _____ to do what He wants. It's 33. _____ who are dumber than animals when it comes to following their Creator.

v. 6-12 Noah and the animals were to wait in the ark for 35. ____ _____ first. Creation scientists believe the flood happened around 36. _____ BC.

The water 'that was above' 37. _____ from the atmosphere and covered the earth, and the 38. _____ water burst through the surface, together combining to flood the entire earth.

The number 40 has become associated with 39. _____ and 40. _____, especially before coming into something 41. _____ and significant.

v. 13-16

v. 17-24 Over 42. _____ cultures have a flood story in their history.

The rains stopped after 43. ____ _____ but the waters from the deep continued to rise for another 44. _____ _____.

Ch 8 v. 1-5 God again 45. _____ ____ _____ to Noah. It wasn't like God had 46. _____ Noah.

v. 6-12 Noah used 47. _____ to test if it was 48. _____ to leave the ark.

v. 13-19 We have the total time Noah was in the ark 49. ____ _____ and ____ days.

v. 20-22 The first thing Noah did was to 50. _____ God and offer a sacrifice for being spared. They 51. _____ God first.

God made a promise that He would never 52. _____ all life on the earth. *Cold and heat, summer and winter* also tells us that there will now be 53. _____ and variations in 54. _____.

Unit 1 The Story Begins
Lesson 6 New Beginning – Same Old Sin
Genesis 9

Essential Question: What were the main changes in people after the flood?

v. 1-7 Noah was to begin the 1. _____ _____ again so he received the same instructions as Adam and Eve. 2. _____

People were now allowed to eat 3. _____. To 4. _____ the animals, God made them naturally 5. _____ of people.

It is used 6. _____ times in 7. _____ separate verses.

- Blood was the sign of 8. _____ for Israel at the first Passover
- Blood sealed God's 9. _____ with Israel
- Blood 10. _____ (made holy) the altar
- Blood 11. _____ _____ the priests
- Blood made 12. _____ for God's people
- Blood 13. _____ the new covenant
- Blood 14. _____ us
- Blood brings 15. _____
- Blood brings 16. _____ with God
- Blood 17. _____ us
- Blood gives 18. _____ to God's holy place
- Blood 19. _____ us
- Blood enables us to 20. _____ Satan

Every human life is also to be 21. _____ for. Because we are made in 22. _____, _____ we are 23. _____ to Him.

v. 8-11 God made a 24. _____ with Noah, his family, his 25. _____, and all living creatures. 26. _____ are Noah's descendants.

- ❖ Covenant - _____
_____.

God's promise was to never again destroy the 27. _____ earth by a flood.

v. 12-17 The rainbow is our 28. _____ still today of God's 29. _____. Every time it rains and a rainbow appears we know God has not 30. _____ His covenant, and He will be 31. _____ to keep it.

V. 18-23 From the sons of Noah: 32. _____, 33. _____, and 34. _____ come all the people on the earth today.

Noah grew a 35. _____. He 36. _____ some of what he made. He drank 37. _____ _____.
Ham's sin was that he not only does not 38. _____ his father, but he also went out and 39. _____ his father.

v. 24-29 Which only proves God made a 40. _____ _____, but man still 41. _____.

Unit 1 The Story Begins
Lesson 7 Babbling at the Tower
Genesis 11:1-9

Essential Question: Why did God scatter the people, and make them spread out over the earth?

v. 1-4 God 1. _____ those coming out of the ark to 2. _____ _____ and subdue the earth. They instead 3. _____ _____ and built a city. They fashioned baked bricks for 4. _____ and used tar as mortar to 5. _____ the tower they were constructing.

All of them building together was not only 6. _____ to God's command, but it also showed they didn't 7. _____ God's promise to never flood the world again.

v. 5-7 God came down—may refer to the person of 8. _____ before He was born to Mary. Let us—refers to the 9. _____.

There is great 10. _____ when sin 11. _____ _____. But separating them showed more of God's 12. _____ than His 13. _____.

Most linguists believe all 14. _____ came from 15. ____ original language.

v. 8-9 The distrust and rebellion against God showed man hadn't gotten any 16. _____ since the flood. God next began to make man better, and He started as He always does: with 17. ____ man who would do His 18. _____, even if he did not do God's will 19. _____.

Name _____

Unit 1 Homework Review #2

1. Who were the first children? _____

2. Why was God pleased with Abel's sacrifice but not Cain's? _____
_____

3. What choice did God give Cain before he went to Abel? _____

4. What happened to Abel? _____

5. What was Cain's punishment? _____

6. What was the problem with the earth during Noah's time? _____
_____

7. What **AND** who did Noah bring with him? _____
_____

8. How long were they in the ark? _____

9. What command did God give both Adam and Eve and Noah and his family? _____
_____

10. What did Ham do after the flood? _____

Unit 1 Verses

Psalms 119:11

I have hidden your word in my heart, that I might not sin against you.

Psalms 9:1-2

I will praise you, O LORD, with all my heart; I will tell of all your wonders. I will be glad and rejoice in you; I will sing praise to your name, O Most High.

Psalms 105:1-3

Give thanks to the LORD, call on his name; make known among the nations what he has done. Sing to him, sing praise to him; tell of all his wonderful acts. Glory in his holy name; let the hearts of those who seek the LORD rejoice.

Jeremiah 29:11

"For I know the plans I have for you," declares the LORD, "plans to prosper you and not to harm you, plans to give you hope and a future."

Genesis 4:6-7

Then the LORD said to Cain, "Why are you angry? Why is your face downcast? If you do what is right, will you not be accepted? But if you do not do what is right, sin is crouching at your door; it desires to have you, but you must rule over it."

Unit 2 God's Nation Begins

Objectives
Students will be able to:
- List the Patriarchs
- Describe the importance of a personal and close relationship with our Creator
- List the promises given to Abraham
- Describe God's plan for a chosen nation
- Describe God's faithfulness to unfaithful humans
- Memorize key passages

Unit Summary

Lesson	Title	Reference
Lesson One	Call of Abraham	Gen. 11:10-12:9
Lesson Two (2)	On Again/Off Again Faithfulness	Gen. 12:10-14:24
Lesson Three	God's Covenant	Gen. 15
Lesson Four	Here Let Me Help	Gen. 16-17
Review 2-1		
Active Lesson	Name of God Art	
Lesson Five	City Lost	Gen. 18-19:29
Lesson Six (2)	Really? A Son at My Age?	Gen. 20-21
Lesson Seven	The Ultimate Test	Gen. 22
Lesson Eight (3)	The Promise Passes	Gen. 23-25:18 and 26
Review 2-2		
Lesson Nine (2)	Squabbling Twins	Gen. 25:19-34 and 27:1-40
Lesson Ten (2)	Finding a New Home and Purpose	Gen. 27:41-29:30
Lesson Eleven (2)	Jacob's Many Blessings	Gen. 29:31-30:24, 35:16-22
Review 2-3		
Lesson Twelve	Wrangling Wages	Gen. 30:25-43
Lesson Thirteen (3)	Home Coming	Gen. 31-33
Lesson Fourteen	Dream a Little Dream	Gen. 37
Lesson Fifteen (3)	God's Bumpy Road	Gen. 39-41
Review 2-4		
Lesson Sixteen (2)	Testing and Changed hearts	Gen. 42-44
Lesson Seventeen	Family Reunion	Gen. 45-46:30
Lesson Eighteen	Foreigners in a Foreign Land	Gen. 46:31-47
Lesson Nineteen (2)	Blessing and Farewells	Gen. 48-49:29 and 50
Review 2-5		

Memory Verses Gen. 12:1-2, Heb. 11:8-9, Gen. 15:16-18, Gen. 41:37-38, Gen. 42:21-22, Gen. 50:20, Prov. 22:3-5

Unit 2 God's Nation Begins
Lesson 1 Call of Abraham
Gen. 11:10-12:9

Essential Question: What is required to be in God's plan?

v. 10-26 The Book of Genesis covers more than 1. _____ years and more than 2. ____ generations. Yet, it spends almost a third of its text on the life of one man – 3. _____.

These verses trace a line from 4. _____, who was blessed, to 5. _____.

† Read James 2:23, 2 Chronicles 20:7, and Isaiah 41:8. What is Abraham called?

_____

v. 27-32 6. "_____". Abram means 7. "_____," Haran means, 8. "_____,_____".

Ch 12:1-3 Chapter 11 is about the plans of 9. _____. Chapter 12 is about the plans of 10. _____.

† What would you do if God told you He wanted you to move out of the Sacramento Valley area—leave your comfortable house to live in the middle of nowhere in a tent for the rest of your life? _____

_____

He didn't 11. _____ Abram's promise away when Abram failed to go where God told him. God put it on 12. _____ until Abram was 13. _____ _____.

How many times in v. 1-3 does God say, "I will…"? ____

God promised to make Abram a 14. _____.

God promised to make Abram's name 15. _____. Today Abram is honored by 16. _____, 17. _____, and 18. _____.

God promised to 19. _____ those who 20. _____ him and 21. _____ those who 22. _____ him.

God promised to make Abram a blessing to 23. _____ _____ _____ of the earth.

v. 4-9 Abram took 24. _____, his nephew, with him.

By building the altar Abram showed:
- ❖ A desire to 25. _____ with God
- ❖ A willingness to offer 26. _____ for sin
- ❖ A desire to 27. _____ to God
- ❖ And a desire to 28. _____ God

Abram lived in a 29. _____ not a permanent resident of the land. We are to live the 30. _____ _____.

Unit 2 God's Nation Begins

Lesson 2 On Again / Off Again Faithfulness
Genesis 12:10-14:24

Essential Questions: What happens when we act in faith to follow God? What happens when we don't? What happens when we do both?

v. 10-13 Abram seemed to believe God would fulfill His promises for the 1. _____, but not that He would fill his 2. _____.

† What do you need to trust God with today? _____
_____

Having Sarai say she was his sister was a 3. _____, but a half-truth is in fact a whole 4. _____. Abram was trying to 5. _____ the Egyptians to save his life, instead of 6. _____ _____ to take care of him.

v. 14-20 Because of Abram's lie, Sarai is put in 7. _____.
God's promise depended on what He 8. _____ _____ —not on what 9. _____ _____.

Ch 13:1-13 Abram's unbelief moved him from his place of 10. _____, and led him into 11. _____. It also caused him to 12. _____ _____ into sin. He learned he could 13. _____ but he didn't trust in the 14. _____ _____ of God. His actions also 15. _____ _____ his family for a while.

Abram was the elder, and the 16. _____ to the land was his alone. Abram also had the 17. _____ to the land because God promised it to him. But here Abram showed his 18. _____ and his 19. _____ in God to provide for him.
We don't have to fight for our 20. _____, God will 21. _____ _____ of us.

Lot picked the land that 22. _____ the best.

Faith is the trust in what we 23. _____ see.

v. 14-18

Ch 14:1-12 But God used this instance to begin to fulfill His promise to Abram—to make his 24. _____ _____ and bless those who 25. _____ him.

v. 13-16 He had his own 26. _____ _____ of 27. _____ trained men.
He used a 28. _____ _____, which was rare for the time, split his men in 29. ____ groups and 30. _____ in rescuing Lot, with the other people, and the stolen plunder.

v. 17-24 He knew if he did, Bera could take 31. _____ for making Abram rich and then use it later to make Abram do his will. Abram wanted God to get the 32. _____ for making him who he was.

† What are you trusting to God and not people? _____
_____

Unit 2 God's Nation Begins
Lesson 3 God's Covenant
Genesis 15

Essential Question: How does God make Himself understandable to His people?

v. 1-3 Abram probably needed to hear he didn't need to 1. _____ because He had defeated a much larger army and maybe expected 2. _____ for his victory. Abram was not 3. _____ to talk to God about what he 4. _____ and his 5. _____. Abram *wanted* to 6. _____, and looked to God to strengthen his 7. _____.

v.4-6 We all need 8. _____. Just because God had promised Abram or us something doesn't mean it will be fulfilled 9. _____ _____. Abram's response was one of complete 10. _____, and God credited him with 11. _____.

v. 7-11 It was clear Abram 12. _____ God, but he asked for 13. _____. Abram was preparing the elements of an ancient 14. _____. In those days anyone could do this when making a covenant, or a 15. "_____ _____" with anyone else. When Abram asked for proof, God didn't get 16. _____.

v. 12-16 Here God did something 17. _____ for Abram. He didn't just give him 18. _____, He also told Abram some of the 19. _____ _____ of his descendants.

v. 17-21 Now God signed the contract with Abram—20. _____. To make a covenant in this fashion 21. _____ people had to walk through the carcasses. God showed Abram, He alone was 22. _____ for keeping His promises to Abram. They would be fulfilled because of Who God 23. _____, not because Abram 24. _____ his end of the 25. _____.

✝ Do you believe God will always keep His promises? Why or why not? _____

_____

Unit 2 God's Nation Begins
Lesson 4 Here Let Me Help
Genesis 16-17

Essential Question: What should you do when it seems like God is not doing what He said He would on your schedule?

v. 1-6 After 1. ____ years in the land, Sarai felt she was the 2. _____.

Just because we wait a long time for God to fulfill or act on our behalf does not mean He 3. _____ _____ act.

- ❖ Abram waited another 4. ____ years for the son of promise
- ❖ Jacob lived in exile for 5. ____ years
- ❖ Moses tended sheep for 6. ____ years before he was called to lead the people out of Egypt.

It is much better to receive God's 7. _____ than to try and 8. _____ Him.

Sarai 9. _____ Abram for the whole mess, though it seems clear it was her 10. _____.

v. 7-16 11. '_____,' appeared to Hagar in the desert. '**The** angel of the Lord' is 12. _____ before He was born to Mary as a God's son on earth.

He said the child's name was to be 13. _____

It is a clear lesson from these chapters of God's Story, that He is a God Who 14. _____ our cries and a God Who 15. _____ our misery.

Ch 17:1-8 16. ____ years passed.

17. _____ _____ —first used here is El-Shaddai in Hebrew. Though it

had been 18. _____ years since God made His promises to Abram, God had not
19. _____ them.

Here God again confirmed with Abram these clear promises:
- ❖ Father of many 20. _____
- ❖ The father of a line of 21. _____
- ❖ An 22. _____ covenant
- ❖ An everlasting possession of the 23. _____ of Canaan

He changed Abram's name (exalted 24. _____) to Abraham (father of 25. _____ _____).

v. 9-14 And God gave Abraham His first instruction for something to 26. _____—circumcision, which was an 27. _____ sign of the covenant between God and His people.

v. 15-16 Sarah was now 28. _____ and the child would come the following year.

v. 17-22 Abraham 29. _____.

v. 23-27 Abraham 30. _____ and was 31. _____ to God's instructions.
People will know what we 32. _____ by our 33. _____.
Abraham's obedience was:

    34. _____ —every male in his household

    35. _____ —that very same day

    36. _____ —wounding all his fighting men on the same day put the camp in danger

Name _____

Unit 2 Homework Review #1

1. Which of Noah's son's was an ancestor of Abraham's? _____

2. Because of the blessing given to Israel (through Abraham) what is one of the reasons America is blessed today? _____

3. According to 1 Peter 2:11 how are we like Abraham? _____

4. Tell a time when Abram showed faith. _____
_____

5. Tell a time when Abram did not show faith. _____
_____

6. What happened between Lot and Abram? _____
_____

7. What did Abram do when Lot got kidnapped? _____
_____

8. Why did Abram refuse to take the reward From the king of Sodom? _____
_____

9. What is a covenant? _____

10. How did God make the covenant with Abram (use lots of details) _____
_____
_____

Unit 2 God's Nation Begins
Lesson 5 City Lost
Genesis 18-19:29

Essential Question: What does compromise do to our witness?

v. 1-5 Less than 1. _____ months had passed since God last spoke with Abraham. The Angel of the Lord (who is 2. _____ before He was born on earth) and 3. _____ angels came to visit Abraham. While Abraham treated his guests with 4. _____ and 5. _____, Sodom was 6. _____ and 7. _____.

8. _____ was brought to wash their feet.
We get the idea that Abraham 9. _____ who his visitors were.

v. 6-8 Abraham prepared a 10. _____ _____ for his honored guests.

v. 9-12 God 11. _____ His promise that 12. _____ would have a son. We need to hear God's 13. _____ repeatedly. God uses repetition to 14. _____ and grow our 15. _____.
The thought of a 90-year-old childless woman suddenly having a child made her 16. _____.

v. 13-15 17. _____ is hidden from God.
God asked if there is 18. _____ too 19. _____ for Him to do.

v. 16-19 There seems to be 20. _____ reasons for God revealing His plan to Abraham. 1.) Wicked Sodom and its neighbor Gomorrah had to be 21. _____ before it had a chance to be 22. _____ through Abraham. 2.) Abraham was to 23. _____ his children righteousness and justice.

v. 20-21

v.22-26 Will God destroy the 24. _____ with the 25. _____?

Abraham's heart was full of 26. _____ and 27. _____.

v. 27-33 Abraham was not trying to talk God into something 28. _____ His will.

Abraham pleaded for 29. _____ for Sodom.

Abraham was 30. _____, and negotiated with God.

Ch 19:1-5 The 31. ____ angels, appearing as men, entered the city. Lot was seen to be

32. _____. He was found sitting at the 33. _____ _____ so

we know he was a 34. _____ _____ in the community.

But Lot was 35. _____. 36. _____ destroyed his 37. _____.

There was nothing 38. _____ about the hospitality Lot offered the visitors. But it

was very unusual to be so 39. _____ in insisting they come to his home.

v. 6-11 Lot himself was only 40. _____ when the angels yanked him back inside and

41. _____ those outside to keep them from breaking down the door.

v. 12-15 Lot has had 42. ____ _____ on anyone in his town.

v.16-22 Lot was so a part of this wicked town that even with the terror he had witnessed, and the

threat of dying with them, Lot 43. _____.

v. 23-29 Lot's wife cared more for the 44. _____ ___ _____ than her own

45. _____. She turned around and turned into a 46. _____ _____ _____.

Lot didn't even have influence on his own 47. _____.

It is clear Lot was 48. _____ out of God's 49. _____ for

50. _____ and not for anything he had done for God.

Unit 2 God's Nation Begins
Lesson 6 Really? A Son at My Age?
Genesis 20-21

Essential Question: Is anything impossible for God?

v.1-2 Abraham again said Sarah was his 1. _____. We should all be mindful of how 2. _____ it is to slip back into 3. _____ _____. Abimelech took Sarah as a 4. _____.

v.3-7 God 5. _____ the king. Even though Abraham did not 6. _____ _____ God again, God did not 7. _____ _____ on him. Only Abraham's 8. _____ saved Abimelech's life.

v. 8-10 Here Abimelech, the foreign king who did not know God, was in the 9. _____, and Abraham, the supposed 10. _____ ____ _____, was in the 11. _____.

v. 11-13 But the real problem was that the 12. _____ _____ _____ wasn't in Abraham. A 13. _____-_____, said with intent to deceive, is always a 14. _____ _____.
This is a way of blaming 15. _____ for the problem.
Abraham should have asked for 16. _____ for dishonoring both the 17. _____ and 18. _____.

v. 14-18 In giving Abraham such great gifts he was adding to Abraham's 19. _____. The additional silver was supposed to 20. "_____ _____ _____."

Ch 21 1-7 It had been 21. ____ years since God made the promise to Abraham about a son, but God fulfilled His promise *at the* 22. _____ _____ *He promised*. Abraham and Sarah respond in 23. _____, named him 24. _____, circumcised him on the 8th day, and 25. _____ God.

God turned a gentle rebuke of Sarah laughing at the thought of having children 26. ____ _____ _____ into an occasion for her great 27. _____ joy.

Isaac is a picture or a foreshadowing of 28. _____

- ❖ Both were the 29. _____ sons.
- ❖ Both were born after a period of 30. _____.
- ❖ Both mothers were assured by God's 31. _____.
- ❖ Both were given 32. _____ rich with meaning 33. _____ they were born.
- ❖ Both births occurred at God's 34. _____ time.
- ❖ Both births were 35. _____.
- ❖ Both births were accompanied by 36. _____

v. 8-13 Abraham was now over 37. _____. Most scholars believe Isaac was about 38. _____. Ishmael was now about 39. _____.

God again 40. _____ the promise would come through 41. _____ and not 42. _____.

v. 14-21 Abraham gave them a 43. _____ _____ and sent them out. Abraham was doing what God led him to do, knowing that 44. _____ God's help, no matter what he gave them, it would not 45. ____ _____; but 46. _____ God, they would have all they needed.

He showed kindness to Ishmael because he was 47. _____ son.

v. 22-34 This ruler notices all the 48. _____ on Abraham's life, and he was smart enough to understand they came from 49. _____. Because it was so clear Abraham's God was with him, this king wanted to make an 50. _____ between them so the blessings could 51. _____ onto him and his people.

Abraham planted a 52. _____ to show he 53. _____ God's provision to keep the tree watered and him 54. _____ in the land.

Unit 2 God's Nation Begins
Lesson 7 The Ultimate Test
Genesis 22

Essential Question: Why does God ask us to do things that seem impossible?

v. 1-2 This was a 1. _____ for Abraham. God asked Abraham to 2. _____ _____ _____. The test was to reveal Abraham's faith. To be real, it had to be 3. _____ what Abraham wanted to do and thought was right.

Because Ishmael was 4. _____ _____ from the family, God considered Abraham to have 5. _____ ____ son. Though the ungodly nations around Abraham practiced child sacrifice, God 6. _____ it. God has never 7. _____ or 8. _____ asked anyone to sacrifice their child.

Here God asked Abraham not to trust the promise but the 9. _____.

v. 3-8 Abraham obeyed, without 10. _____, complaint, discussion with others, stalling, or apparent worry. Now Abraham could obey, and trust even when he didn't 11. _____.

† Tell about a time in the past or now when you had to trust God even though you didn't understand, or didn't feel like it _____
_____

The distance between Beersheba and Mount Moriah (modern day 12. _____) was about 13. ____ miles and was a 14. ____ day journey. 15. _____ are going to worship and 16 _____ will come back.

God said the promises given would come through 17. _____ and God never 18. _____ and B) God wanted 19. _____ sacrificed.

Isaac, the 20. ____ _____ _____ beloved son, carried his own 21. _____ on his 22. _____ up a 23. _____. Does this remind you of anyone? _____

Walking Law and History: Genesis/ 42

v. 9-11 Remember, at this time Abraham is over 24. ____, and Jewish scholars think Isaac could have been in his 25. _____. While everyone remembers 26. _____ faith in willingly offering his son and trusting God with the results, we can't forget the faith of 27. _____ in allowing his father to tie him to the altar.

Always remember: God often looks at the 28. _____ _____ over the actual 29. _____.

v. 12-14 The words here sound very much like another well-known verse. Can you name it? _____

God still wanted a 30. _____. He provided a 31. _____ in place of Isaac.

Worship involved 32. _____ God's sacrificial substitute. In the New Testament God 33. _____ the perfect sacrifice for the animal: His only Son.

Isaac's picture of 34. _____ becomes even clearer:

- ❖ Both were 35. _____ by their father.
- ❖ Both offered themselves 36. _____.
- ❖ Both 37. _____ _____ up the hill of their sacrifice.
- ❖ Both were delivered from death on the 38. _____ day.

v. 15-19 A rough calculation of the numbers of stars and grains of sand is believed to be about the same. Scientist believe it is about 39. ____ to the 40. _____ power.

v. 20-24 A 41. _____ was a special kind of wife. A concubine had to 42. _____ the real wife.

- † Have you ever known that God wanted to bless you or wanted to give you something amazing and you saw someone else get it first? _____
- † How did it make you feel? _____
- † How did it affect your relationship with God? _____

_____

Unit 2 God's Nation Begins
Lesson 8 The Promise Passes
Genesis 23-25:18 and 26

Essential Question: How do we fit into God's complete plan?

v. 1 The only 1. _____ in the Bible whose 2. _____ _____ _____ is recorded, is Sarah. It shows us how 3. _____ she was in God's plan.

Never are we told to look to 4. _____ as an example of a godly woman. But 5. _____ we are told to look to 6. _____ as an example.

v. 2 Abraham was man enough to 7. _____ and mourn the loss of his beloved wife.

v. 3-16 Abraham was 8. _____ among his neighbors. We are all 9. _____ on this earth, not just when we travel some place new.

Abraham showed us how believers should do business: 10. _____, 11. _____, and 12 _____.

v. 17-20 This first 13. _____ of the patriarchs.

Ch. 24 God ensured the 14. _____ of His promise by guiding Abraham's servant to His chosen 15. _____ for Isaac.

v. 1-4 Abraham has his honored servant place his hand under his 16. _____. It was a very serious 17. _____ showing us how 18. _____ it was to Abraham that Isaac 19. ____ _____ a local Canaanite girl.

v. 5-9 Abraham made sure his servant clearly 20. _____ all he was to do in case Abraham should 21. _____ before Isaac's bride arrived.

v.10-16 The servant trusted in 22. _____. He prayed and asked God for a 23. _____ _____ of the woman God had chosen for Isaac. He is wise enough to ask for a sign that would be 24. _____.
It seems like the servant didn't care what this bride 25. _____ like. He wanted a woman of 26. _____ that God had chosen. God 27. _____ the servant's request 28. _____ he was finished praying.

v. 17-21 Maybe he was watching to see if Rebekah would just 29. _____ a good talk or if she really had a 30. _____ _____ and would do all of the hard work until it was 31. _____ without 32. _____.

v. 22-27 He 33. _____ Rebekah for her labor with 34. _____. She was so kind she not only offered him a 35. _____, but also offered to 36. _____ his camels too.

v. 28-33 Laban 37. _____ to meet the man who had just showered his sister in gold. He offered all the 38. _____ he could.

v. 34-49 He said he had to tell them 39. _____ _____ first.

v. 50-54 The servant bowed in 40. _____ to 41. _____ when Laban and Rebekah's father agree to the marriage. Then he gave both 42. _____ and her 43. _____ gifts.

v. 55-60 The servant prepared to 44. _____ the next day with Rebekah. Laban and her mother tried to 45. _____ his departure.
Laban suggested they ask Rebekah's 46. _____.

Rebekah surprised them all by saying without hesitation, "I 47. _____ go."

They sent Rebekah off with 48. _____, praying God would give her thousands of strong and powerful 49. _____.

v. 61-67 Rebekah 50. _____ her face before meeting her new husband.

The way Isaac and Rebekah met each other is a good picture of how 51. _____ and the 52. _____ come together.

- A father desired a 53. _____ for his son.
- A son was just accounted as 54. "_____" and "raised from the dead"
- Abraham's servant's name was *Eliezer*, meaning "God of 55. _____"
- The lovely bride was 56. _____ met, chosen, and called, and then 57. _____ with gifts.
- She was entrusted to the 58. _____ of the servant until she met her 59. _____. (Holy Spirit)

Both Isaac and 60. _____:

- Were 61. _____ before their coming.
- Finally appeared at the 62. _____ time.
- Were conceived and born 63. _____.
- Given a special 64. _____ before birth.
- Offered up in 65. _____ by the father.
- Brought back from the 66. _____.
- Head of a great company to 67. _____ all people.
- Prepared a place for their 68. _____.
- Had a ministry of 69. _____ while the bride comes.

Both 70. _____ *and the church:*

Walking Law and History: Genesis/ 46

- ❖ Chosen for marriage 71. _____ they knew it.
- ❖ 72. _____ for the accomplishment of God's eternal 73. _____.
- ❖ Destined to share in the 74. _____ of the son.
- ❖ Learned about the son through his 75. _____.
- ❖ Must leave 76. _____ with joy to be with the son.
- ❖ Are 77. _____ and 78. _____ _____ by the son.

Throughout this story we see the hand of 79. _____.
- ❖ God was the sole 80. _____ of all the events in the story.
- ❖ God was deliberately 81. _____ the _____ directing the acts.
- ❖ Not chance or luck, but clearly part of God's 82. _____ to 83. _____ the world

Ch 25:1-4 They had many 84. _____ together, and we will see some of these sons become 85. _____ that Israel will run into throughout their history.

v. 5-6 Abraham was 86. _____ to make sure Isaac, received all that he had.

v. 7-11 His faithfulness is honored as he is talked about in 87, ___ verses of the New Testament.

v. 12-18

(skip to chapter 26. Come back to 25:19 next lesson)

26:1-6 Here God 88. _____ Isaac when another famine swept across the land. Here God gave the same promises 89. _____ to Isaac.

v. 7-10 Here we go again. Isaac goes from the 90. _____ of hearing from God to a 91. _____ sin.

Walking Law and History: Genesis/ 47

† Has this ever happened to you? Have you spent time with God in deep worship or prayer and felt really close to Him, then done a big sin—lied to your parents, cheated on a test, gossiped about a friend? _____

Satan loves to hit us when we are feeling the 92. _____.

Isaac said Rebekah was his 93. _____.

v. 11 Like God did for his father, Abraham, God 94. _____ Isaac, Rebekah, and His plans for the future.

v. 12-15 God 95. _____ Isaac's hard work with 96. _____ times more than he had planted. His 97. _____ multiplied too. They were so 98. _____ they threw dirt in all the wells Abraham had dug. But no matter what man did, they couldn't stop the 99. _____ _____ _____.

v. 16-22 It is not God's desire that we live in 100. _____ and 101. _____.

v. 23-25 God again met with Isaac and 102. _____ the _____. And Isaac did as his father, and 103. _____ an _____ and 104. _____.

v. 26-33 Like the king of the past, this Abimelech made a 105. _____ _____ _____ with Isaac. He could see God's hand on this man and wanted to share in the 106. _____.

† Is God's power in your life strong enough to draw other people to you just so they can share in what God is doing for you? _____
† Do you want it to be that way? _____

Name _____

Unit 2 Homework Review #2

1. Why did God change Abram's name to Abraham? _____
   _____

2. Who is "The Angel of the Lord?" _____

3. List the things Abraham did to make his guests feel welcome. _____
   _____

4. When God told Abraham His plans for Sodom and Gomorrah, what did Abraham ask? _____

5. Describe what affect Lot had on his city and family for God. _____
   _____

6. Why did God choose Isaac as the boy's name? _____
   _____

7. How old was Abraham when Isaac was born? _____

8. What happened to Hagar and Ishmael? _____

9. What did God ask Abraham to do with Isaac? _____

10. How was Isaac saved? _____

Unit 2 God's Nation Begins
Lesson 9 Squabbling Twins
Genesis 25:19-34, 26:34-35, and 27:40

Essential Question: How are God's ways different than man's ways?

v. 19-26 Isaac, though the son of Promise, did not get his promise without 1. _____ and 2. _____. Isaac and Rebekah waited 3. _____ years before they had their only children, twin boys. When she didn't understand what was happening to her, she went and asked 4. _____.

God's answer was clear. "You are going to have 5. _____. Both will be great 6. _____ and the 7. _____ will serve the 8. _____."

She named the boys by what was seen when they were born.

Esau – 9. _____ _____ _____

Jacob – 10. _____

These two warred in the 11. _____, while 12. _____ _____, and their descendants even warred throughout their 13. _____.

v. 27-28 Isaac loved 14. _____ more, and Rebekah loved 15. _____ more.

v. 29-34 The 16. _____ was very 17. _____. It dealt with both the 18. _____ inheritance and the 19. _____ _____ of the father. Jacob 20. _____ it, and he was going to 21. _____ Esau out of it.

Esau showed no 22. _____ or 23. _____ for what was his by the right of being born first in God's plan. Esau chose the 24. _____ _____ of a full belly over the 25. _____ _____ of great wealth.

☦ Is there something small you are now fighting for while giving up something greater in the future? _____

Jacob made Esau 26. _____ he would get the birthright. He was scheming to get what God had 27. _____ said was his. Therefore Esau was selling something that was 28. _____ _____ to begin with.

Ch 26:34-35 We continue to see Esau's 29. _____ for his family and God. He married two Hittite women, and they brought 30. _____ to his parents.

Ch 27:1-4 This whole chapter is about people 31. _____ in their own 32. _____ for their own 33. _____, and not in God's 34. _____ according to His 35. _____.
He must have 36. _____ what God told his wife, Rebekah, about the older serving the younger, but he hoped to 37. _____ _____ God's back and bless his favorite son.

v. 5-12 Rebekah 38. _____ what Isaac planned, and put Jacob to work to 39. _____ her husband into giving the 40. _____ to the 41. _____ son. He didn't feel 42. _____ about tricking his father, just 43. _____ he was going to get caught doing it.

v. 13-17 We cannot 44. _____ _____ the truth of what is right and what is wrong for 45. _____ _____. Because in our own strength nothing works as it is supposed to. No one in this story was doing 46. _____ _____. Isaac could have given Esau 100 blessings, but they would only matter if God Almighty 47. _____ them.

v. 18-29 Jacob clearly 48. _____ to his father. And he brought God into it by saying "I had great luck hunting because God gave me the success." This was dangerous. Isaac questioned his identity 49. _____ times, but when Jacob 50. _____ hairy like his brother, and 51. _____ like his brother Isaac trusted his 52. _____, and gave the blessing.

The blessing included:
- ❖ Prosperity in 53. _____
- ❖ Domination over other 54. _____ and his 55. _____
- ❖ 56. _____ for those who cursed him
- ❖ 57. _____ for those who blessed him

v. 30-38 Esau 58. _____ with his prize and in excitement prepared it and took it to his father.

He was hopping mad. He had been 59. _____ into doing what God 60. _____ done in the first place. God's perfect will had 61. _____ and Isaac must 62. _____ it. So must 63. _____.

Then we see Esau's 64. _____ _____, he 65. _____ for a blessing too. Though he thoughtlessly 66. _____ his birthright for a bowl of soup now Esau said Jacob 67. _____ it from him as well as the blessing. Now the birthright meant something to him. At first Esau saw the birthright as 68. _____, and it had no value for him, but when he saw the 69. _____ and 70. _____ benefits of the birthright, he wanted it.

Esau's tears were tears of frustrated 71. _____. He didn't 72. _____ his sin and the despising of his birthright; just what he lost in not getting the inheritance.

v. 39-40 Because the rich, dew covered ground had been promised to 73. _____, it couldn't also be given to 74. _____.

Unit 2 God's Nation Begins
Lesson 10 Finding a New Home and Purpose
Gen. 27:41-29:30

Essential Question: How can God use the hard times in our lives?

v. 41-46 Isaac's family was 1. _____ _____. Esau went along with the plan, 2. _____ his agreement with Jacob to give up the birthright. Both Rebekah and Jacob tried to 3. _____ God's blessings through 4. _____.

Now Esau threatened to 5. _____ Jacob as soon as his father died. The thought of killing his brother 6. _____ Esau. Rebekah had Isaac send him away under the ploy of finding a 7. _____.

Ch 28. 1-5 Isaac now did what he was suppose to. He 8. _____ Jacob 9. _____ and then he gave him some 10. _____. It was very important Jacob did 11. _____ _____ a Canaanite woman like his brother. He had the birthright and the 12. _____ would pass to him. He would be an ancestor of the 13. _____. We see the blessing of Abraham, 14. _____, 15. _____, and 16. _____, passed now to Jacob.

v. 6-9 So in a vain attempt to 17. _____ to his father he was also 18. _____ of praise and blessing, Esau marries a half-cousin: 19. _____ daughter. Clearly Esau had no understanding of the requirements for 20. _____ within the covenant of Abraham.

v. 10-15 Not because of Jacob's 21. _____, but because of God's 22. _____ and 23. _____, God confirmed the blessing and the 24. _____ with Jacob.

The ladder between heaven and earth told Jacob, God was 25. _____.

God would be 26. _____ him as he traveled outside his land of promise, and would see to his safe 27. _____.

This is an important goal of God throughout the Bible. God 28. _____ His people and promised them 29. _____ and 30. _____ so that they could then be a 31. _____ to others.

v. 16-19 Jacob 32. _____ his loyalty to God and he 33. _____. His worship included:
- Having 34 34. _____ before the Lord
- Setting up a 35. _____ stone or pillar
- Making it holy with 36. _____
- Naming the place 37. _____ ___ _____
- Promising to 38. _____

It was not the 39. _____ that was important, but 40. _____ filled it.

v. 20-22 God had given Jacob an amazing 41. _____, yet he was still trying to make 42. _____.

† Are you the same way? Are God's words not enough? Do you need to see before you will believe? _____
_____

There was a huge difference between God's 43. _____ and Jacob's 44. _____.

God promised
- *I am the* 45. _____ _____.

- *I will 46. _____ to you.*
- *I am 47. _____ you.*
- *I will not 48. _____ you until I have done what I have spoken.*

Jacob's vow:
- 49. _____ _____ will be with me.
- And 50. _____ me.
- In this way that 51. _____ _____ going.
- 52. _____ ____ bread and clothing.
- So that I 53. _____ _____ to my father's house.

Ch 29:1-3 Jacob 54. _____ his encounter with God and 55. _____ on his journey (literally 56. "_____" to his relatives home. God's 57. _____ with him and allowed him to arrive 58. _____ to a well in their town.

v. 4-9 He quickly learned he was at his 59. _____, and these men knew his 60. _____.

Jacob 61. _____ to find a well. The well 62. _____ to be near the town of Haran where Laban lived. And while he was standing there Rachel 63. _____ to come to water her father's sheep. Obviously this was all God 64. ____ _____ behind the scenes. It has been said that a 65. _____ is when God chooses to remain 66. _____.

In the Bible, wells are often associated with God's 67. _____.

v. 10-14a Laban's shepherds appear to be 68. _____, while Jacob came across as 69. _____, 70. _____, and 71. _____-_____.

Jacob greeted his cousin with a 72. _____ Then he 73. _____ for joy at the success of his long journey.

Laban again 74. _____ _____ to meet him, and now greeted Jacob and invited him 75. _____.

Though we don't read about God's 76. _____ involvement in Jacob finding Rachel it is clearly 77. _____.

v. 14b-20 Laban asked Jacob what he wanted his 78. _____ to be. Jacob was the son of a very 79. _____ man. But for now, he had to 80. _____ as a lowly hired hand, and while he was probably not a lazy man, he never had to do the 81. _____ _____ he would now have to do.

Jacob offered to work for 82. ____ years to marry Rachel. While Jacob came from a very wealthy family, he left home 83. _____ in an attempt to escape his brother's anger. Men were expected to pay a 84. _____.

Jacob's 85. _____ for Rachel was so great his seven years only felt like 86. _____. True love 87. _____.

v. 21-25 Now the 88. _____ had been 89. _____. Jacob was the 90. _____, and took the place of his 91. _____ brother. Laban gave his 92. _____ daughter in marriage in place of the 93. _____.

When we are 94. _____ to what God wants us to do, it may not effect God's plans, but it will change how we end up 95. _____ our life.

v. 26-30 Jacob promised to work 96. _____ seven years to marry his love. Jacob clearly 97. _____ one of his wives 98. _____ than the other.

Unit 2 God's Nation Begins
Lesson 11 Jacob's Many Blessings
Gen. 29:31-30:24 and 35:16-22

Essential Question: How did God build the nation of Israel?

v. 31-32 God saw Leah's 1. _____. He knew she was not 2. _____ by her husband, but God loved her greatly and gave her what was the 3. _____ _____ for a woman of the day. She gave birth to many 4. _____.

Rachel could not have 5. _____. She had her husband's 6. _____ but not the honor of being a 7. _____.

Leah's oldest son was 8. _____. His name sounds like a word that means 9. "_____ _____ _____ _____", and said, *Surely my husband will 10. _____ me now.* Jacob's favor and love on only one wife made Leah 11. _____. These 12. _____ trapped her in a terrible situation, but God 13. _____ her.

v. 33 Leah had another son, because God heard her husband still did not 14. _____ her. She called him 15. _____ meaning 16. "_____ _____ _____."

v. 34 Leah had a third son and named him 17. _____ meaning, 18. "_____." "He may not love me, but now that I have given him three beautiful sons, Jacob will at least be 19. _____ to me."

v. 35 Then Leah had a fourth son. His name was 20. _____ meaning, 21. "_____." She had 22. _____ _____ on her husband loving her or even being attached to her. She turned to the only One who had 23. _____ her 24. _____ and 25. _____ His name.

It seems as though Leah was 26. _____ by Jacob and 27. _____ by

Rachel. But God had a great 28. _____ for her. The two 29. _____ tribes came from Leah. 30. _____ (the 31. _____ tribe) and 32. _____ (the 33. _____ tribe). But most important, the 34. _____ was Leah's great, great, great… grandson. Leah, learned to look to the 35. _____ and praise Him.

Ch 30: 1-3 Rachel, though 36. _____ and very 37. _____, was 38. _____ of her sister and near 39. _____.

Leah wanted to be 40. _____. Rachel wanted 41. _____.

† Do you compare yourself to others? _____

† What do you wish God would give you or change about you? _____
_____

† Pray about this. Ask God to make you content with who He has made you to be and with what He has given you.

Rachel in desperation did as Sarah, and offered her husband 42. _____ _____.

v. 4-6 Out of love for his hurting wife, Jacob 43. _____ and Bilhah had a son for Rachel to raise. Rachel named him 44. _____ meaning "He has 45. _____."

v. 7-8 Bilhah had another son for Rachel and he was named 46. _____ meaning, 47. "_____." Rachel declared she had 48. _____ over her sister.

v. 9-11 Leah saw her sister 49. _____ at her two surrogate sons and threw her servant Zilpah in the mix and made her 50. _____ _____ of Jacob.

Zilpah gave Leah another son for Jacob. Leah named him 51. _____, 52. "_____ _____."

v. 12-13 Leah was 53. _____ when Zilpah had another son for her. His name was 54. _____ meaning, 55. "_____." But in saying *The women will call me happy* it appears she was more interested in her 56. _____ among the other women of her community than the 57. _____ himself.

v. 14-18 Reuben was older now and found a 58. _____ _____.

Rachel 59. _____ for this mystic root. We don't see her 60. _____, but she was willing to try 61. _____.

Leah's response was 62. _____.

Rachel 63. _____ to let Jacob go to Leah's tent that night in 64. _____ for the root.

Is there any wonder why God said a man should only marry 65. ____ _____?

Later, when God gave the laws, He forbid marrying 66. ____ _____.

Leah again had a child. She gave Jacob another son 67. _____, 68. "_____."

v. 19-21 Leah had another son 69. _____, 70. "_____." She said this son was a 71. _____ _____ from God, and maybe her husband would at least 72. _____ her.

Notice this trapped woman's journey from hoping her husband would 73. _____ her, to wanting him to be 74. _____ to her, to finally just wanting him to 75. _____ her.

Then Leah had a 76. _____. How must it have been for 77. _____?

v. 22-24 God had not 78. _____ Rachel just as He had not forgotten 79. _____ in the ark. He now turned His 80. _____ to her and allowed her to have a 81. _____. She 82. _____ God for a son of her own saying, *God has taken away my* 83. _____. She named him 84. _____, "may He 85. _____" showing she hoped God would give her 86. _____ children.

God will use this 87- _____ son to save his 88. _____ and to carry out His plan.

Ch 35:16-18 Once they returned to the land of 89. _____, Rachel became pregnant again. She named him 90. _____-_____ "son of my 91. _____." Jacob did not want to remember the 92. _____ of his beloved wife every time he said his son's name, so he re-named him 93. _____, "son of my 94. _____ _____."

In the Bible the right side is associated with greater 95. _____ and 96. _____.

v. 19-20 Earlier we saw Rachel plead for 97. _____ or she would die. Now we see it was in fact the having of a child that 98. _____ her.

She received all her 99. _____ during her life. Her honor lives on 100. _____ _____.

Name _____

Unit 2 Homework Review #3

In the large rectangle write the name of each of Jacob's sons by that mother. In the small squares put the number for the order of the boy's birth.

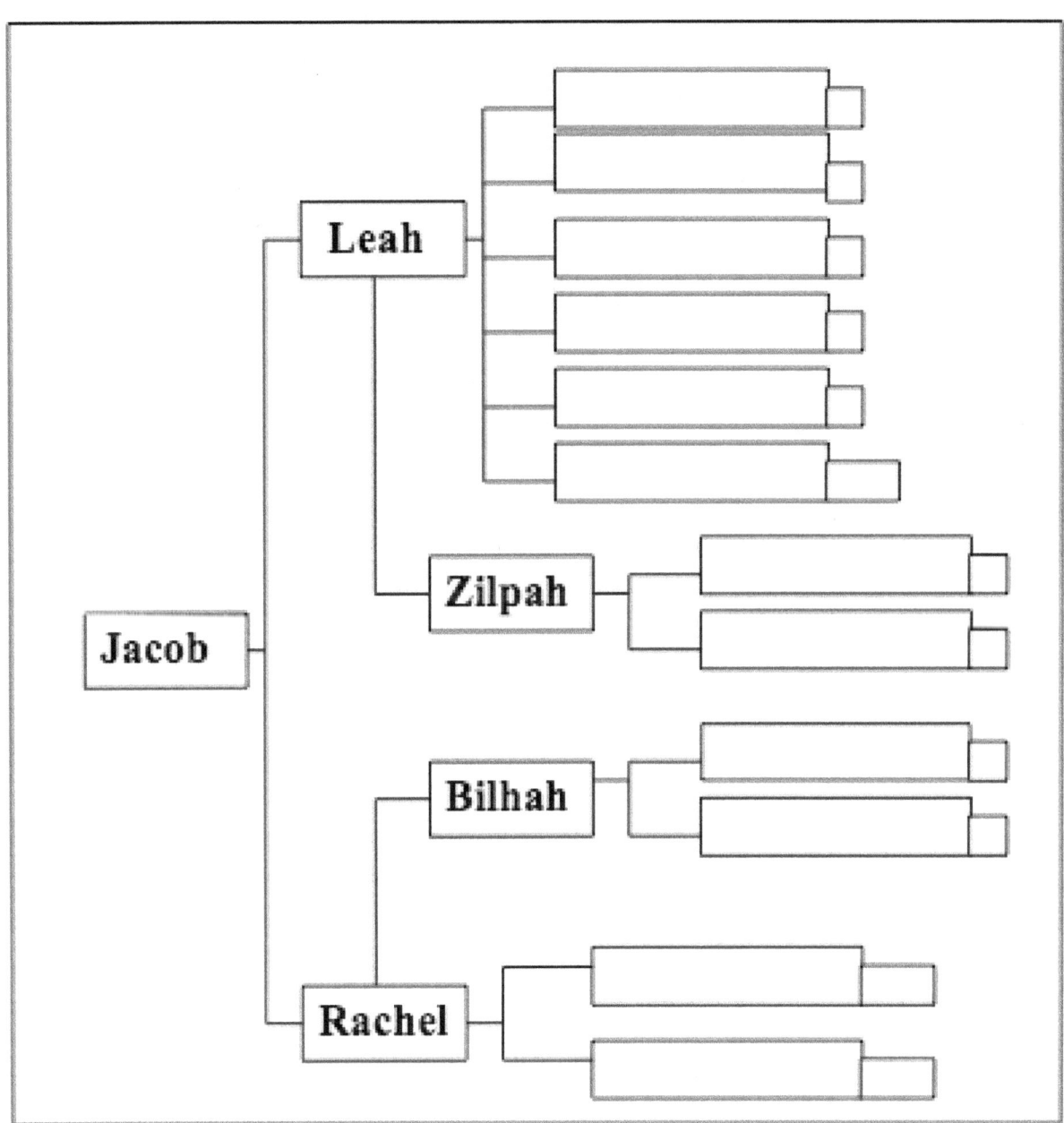

Name _____

Jacob's 13 and Counting

ACROSS
2. Jacob's only daughter.
5. He was a precious gift to his mother.
7. Born to Leah by Zilpah his name meant good fortune.
8. His mother thought he was her reward.
10. Leah's third son, the one she hoped would make Jacob attached to her.
11. Named because Jacob did not love his mother, but God heard.
12. The oldest son of Jacob's favorite wife.

DOWN
1. Rachel thought this child made her a winner.
2. The son born to Rachel by Bilhah who took away her shame.
3. The youngest son. His birth caused his mother's death.
4. Leah gave up on Jacob and praised God for the gift of this son.
6. Leah was so happy about this son she said everyone will call me happy.
9. The oldest son.

Unit 2 God's Nation Begins
Lesson 12 Wrangling Wages

Essential Question: Who is ultimately in control of our wealth and processions?

v. 25-26 Jacob had worked for 1. _____ for fourteen years, and now that his debt of the 2. _____ had been paid, he wanted to return 3. _____. He asked his father-in-law for 4. _____ to leave, and reminded Laban of all the 5. _____ _____ he had done for him.

v. 27-28 Laban asked him to 6. _____ saying the crystal ball said he had only been 7. _____ because of 8. _____.

v. 29-33 Jacob reminded Laban how 9. _____ he had become because of his hard work. Now he wanted to start gaining his 10. _____ _____. Jacob didn't want Laban to give him a 11. ____ _____ payment. He wanted to earn a 12. _____ _____ from now on and set the terms of their contract. If Laban agreed, Jacob would 13. _____ to oversee the care of all Laban's livestock.

Jacob asked for all the 14. _____ and 15. _____ sheep and the 16. _____ _____ lambs and goats born in Laban's flocks.

Then from that day forward, any 17. _____ or 18. _____ born spotted, speckled, or dark in Laban's flocks would become 19. _____.

v. 34-36 Laban quickly 20. _____ to the deal. It was a very easy way to tell the two men's flocks 21. _____, and it seemed Jacob was giving Laban the 22. _____.

As Jacob 23. _____ his work of caring for his father-in-law's flocks, Laban

24. _____ all the multicolored animals from his flocks. Laban's sons then took these goats and sheep a 25. _____ journey away.

v. 37-43 Jacob did a 26. _____ of different things to make his flocks 27. _____.

This made his flock 28. _____ and 29. _____ and Laban's 30. _____ and 31. _____.

Even with all Jacob's 32. _____ and 33. _____, it was 34. _____ Who blessed him and made him 35. _____.

Unit 2 God's Nation Begins
Lesson 13 Home Coming
Gen. 31-33

Essential Question: How can fear affect the promises God has for us?

v. 1-3 Jacob did not take 1. _____ away from Laban. When he was earning a wage, 2. _____ made him very 3. _____. Laban was not losing anything. His flocks were 4. _____ too, but Laban's sons were 5. _____ of Jacob.

When you are 6. _____ it is hard to see the 7. _____. Jealousy is a 8. _____. God shows us there is a 9. _____ way.

✝ What is the better way? _____

God told him it was now time to go 10. _____. God led Jacob in a way He often leads us:
- Jacob 11. _____ to go home (Gen. 30:25)
- His current situation became so 12. _____ he couldn't stay
- God gave him 13. _____.

Clearly God 14. _____ _____ Jacob at all times. Seeing how God 15. _____ for and 16. _____ Jacob should help us to know God will do the 17. _____ for us. God never 18. _____.

v. 4-13 Jacob called his 19. _____ out to meet him and told them how things had been for him. But Jacob chose to speak with them honestly about the situation so they would also 20. _____ to come with him. Jacob gave all the 21. _____ to God.

God told Jacob to return to his home, to 22. _____ were he first encountered God in a personal way. By going back to the places where God did 23. _____ _____ for us we remember God will 24. _____ to meet all our needs.

v. 14-16 Moving this huge family of two 25. _____, two 26. _____, eleven 27. _____, one 28. _____, and unknown numbers of servants and livestock would have been like moving a small 29. _____.
There was 30. _____ _____ for them with their father.
Notice both the wives 31. _____ together.

v. 17-21 Jacob waited until his father-in-law was 32. _____ with the sheep shearing, packed up his family, and 33. _____ away. God 34. _____ him to go, and 35. _____ he would be safe. Jacob trusted, but only a little.
Rachel stole her father's 36. _____.

v. 22-24 Laban 37. _____ about Jacob's departure and gathered a gang of men, his posse, and 38. _____ after them. The night before they met, God 39. _____ Laban. That makes scholars believe Laban probably 40. _____ to harm Jacob. Even though Jacob sneaked away, God still 41. _____ him.

v. 25-30 42. He was a _____.
43. He resorted to _____ _____.
44. He _____.
45. And he _____ Jacob.

v. 31-35 Jacob denied having the idols. He clearly didn't know 46. _____ had taken them, because he promised whomever was found with them would be put to 47. _____.

v. 36-42 But Jacob was not just angry about this 48. _____. He took Laban to task about all the 49. _____ he had suffered while living with him like a slave.

Jacob reported:

- ❖ Your animals have not 50. _____.
- ❖ I 51. _____ none of your livestock.
- ❖ I gave you one of my live 52. _____ every time a wild beast ate one of yours.
- ❖ And I had to 53. _____ every time one of your flock was stolen.
- ❖ I tended your flocks 54. _____ and_____, 55. _____ and _____, and going without 56. _____.
- ❖ I worked for 57. _____ years for my wives (only one of which I wanted).
- ❖ And another 58. _____ for my flocks. Yet, you changed my wages 59. ten times.

v. 43-50 Laban again tried to work things out for his 60. _____ _____, claiming "All these are 61. _____!

v. 51-55 Laban suggested a 62. _____.

After the covenant agreement between them, they 63. _____ _____.

Ch 32: 1-2 These protecting angels had 64. _____ _____ with Jacob, it was just now that he 65. _____ them.

Spiritual 66. _____ goes on around us all the time, but we can't see it.

v. 3-6 Jacob got a message from 67. _____, and then sent a message to his 68. _____. Jacob was not coming home to claim his 69. _____. Jacob called himself Esau's 70. _____. But when he learned his brother was coming to meet him, it didn't appear to be a 71. _____ _____ as his brother was coming with 72. _____ men. Jacob could only assume this was Esau's 73. _____ _____, and was 74. _____ for the lives of his family.

v. 7-8 Jacob was terrified. This was the opposite of his reaction to Laban when he confronted Jacob with his small army. Jacob did not feel 75. _____ in his actions with Laban, but he felt very 76. _____ in how he had treated his brother.

† Is there anything you are feeling guilty about? _____

† Have you asked God to forgive you? _____

† What are you going to do to stop feeling guilty and live as God wants you to?
_____

Jacob did everything 77. _____ possible to save his family, or at least some of it. He didn't stop to 78. _____, but he 79. _____ his family.

v. 9-12 Now Jacob 80. _____.

† Do you pray using words from Scripture? _____

Maybe it is time to add Scripture to part of your prayer time.

Jacob showed he understood the situation for what it was. He was only 81. _____ and 82. _____ because of God. He did not deserve God's 83. _____, but Jacob knew if he was to 84. _____ it would only be because of God acting on his 85. _____. Even his prayer and repeating God's promises didn't make Jacob 86. _____ any better.

Too often we trust our 87. _____ over what we know is 88. _____ about God and His character.

v. 13-21 He sent a 89. _____ of his 90. _____ from God as a gift for his brother. A total of 91. _____ animals, not counting the baby camels.

v. 22-26 Jacob now showed some 92. _____ by sending his family and all his possessions 93. _____ across the river.

Jacob's nightlong 94. _____ struggle is much like us struggling with God to get our 95. _____ or our attempt to force God to do what we want. It is never a 96. _____ fight. God is so much more 97. _____ than us. We 98. _____ win over God.

† What are you struggling about with God in hopes of getting your own way?
_____

The match between Jacob and the Man seemed 99. _____. But it only seemed that way because the Man didn't choose to defeat Jacob 100. _____.

There is a lot to 101. _____ in our struggles with God. God uses the 102. _____ for His many purposes.

Jacob had clearly 103. _____. He could not continue to 104. _____ with such an injury, but he still 105. _____ to the Man.

Jacob recognized God was 106. _____, just as we must all know we serve a God who is greater than us. "We cannot 107. _____ much of anything until He 108. _____ us."

Now God 109. _____ his prayer. Before God could save Jacob from Esau, God had to save Jacob from his trust in what he could do. Jacob's real enemy was 110. _____.

v. 27-29 The Man asked Jacob's 111. _____. God gave him a new name, 112. _____. This new name fit Jacob because he had fought with 113. _____ for the birthright, and he had struggled against 114. _____ for control over his own life. But it also showed that God would 115. _____ for Israel.

To say that Jacob *had* 116. _____ did not mean that he 117. _____ God. You only 118. _____ with God by 119. _____ your own will, but not 120. _____ _____ until you accept God's 121. _____.

v. 30-32 Jacob was 122. _____ in his physical body, but bold in 123. _____.

Ch 33:1-3 Jacob lined up his 124. _____.

Jacob went 125. _____ of his family, took a step, 126. _____ all the way to the ground, 127. ____ times. Showing not only did he not want any of Esau's 128. _____ he also didn't want to be the 129. _____ of the family.

v. 4-7 Esau 130. _____ to 131. _____ his brother.

v. 8-11 Jacob called himself Esau's 132. _____ and referred to Esau as 'My lord'. Esau, however, called Jacob 133. '_____.

Jacob insisted that he take the 134. _____ and the 135. _____ as a way to show that he was 136. _____. When Esau accepted, he showed he had 137. _____ Jacob.

Both men testified to God's great 138. _____. *I have* 139. _____.

v. 12-17 It seemed that while Jacob was 140. _____ that his brother did not wish him dead any longer he still didn't 141. _____ Esau. But Jacob showed he was still Jacob the 142. _____ for while Esau headed 143. _____ toward home, Jacob turned 144. _____.

v. 18-20 Jacob came to the very place where his grandfather, 145. _____, first 146. _____ when he arrived in Canaan. He also bought a piece of 147. _____, like Abraham, and made an 148. _____ to worship God.

Jacob made a 149. _____ settlement in Shechem. This lack of 150. _____ caused Jacob trouble.'

Unit 2 God's Nation Begins
Lesson 14 Dream a Little Dream
Gen. 37

Essential Question: What reactions do God's gifts sometimes cause in others?

God's story in Genesis now turns to one of Jacob's 1. _____. It is another wonderful example of 2. _____. This son was a 3. _____ and 4. _____ star among his brothers, and an 5. _____ of faith for all of us.

"Enoch showed the 6. _____ of faith, Noah showed the 7. _____ of faith, Abraham showed the 8. _____ of faith, Isaac showed the 9. _____ of faith, and Jacob showed the 10. _____ of faith. Along these lines we could say that Joseph showed the 11. _____ of faith. Joseph never 12. _____ and he never 13. _____."

Joseph is one of the best examples and pictures of 14. _____ we have in all the Old Testament.

v. 1-4 Joseph was 15. _____, and while he worked with the rest of his brothers, he seemed to be a bit of a 16. _____-_____. While he was 17. _____ to his father, this action no doubt made him no 18. _____ among his brothers.

It also let everyone know Joseph was not only 19. _____ over the others, but a 20. _____ among his brothers and the one who would receive the 21. _____.

v. 5-8 Telling them he would 22. _____ _____ them and that they would 23. _____ at his feet wasn't a wise choice.
The brothers didn't 24. _____ the meaning of the dream.

v. 9-11 Joseph had another 25. _____. In the ancient world the image of the sun, moon, and stars represented 26. _____ and 27. _____. This dream not only showed Joseph above his 28. _____ but also above his 29. _____. Joseph was the 30. _____, got special 31. _____, and received 32. _____ about the future.

Jacob 33. _____ Joseph, and his brothers' 34. _____, and 35. _____ grew to the point where they 36. _____ against him.

v. 12-18 From the Valley of Hebron where Jacob and his family lived it was about 37. ____ miles north. It would take Joseph between 39. _____ hours of straight walking to get to his brothers.

v. 19-22 His brothers had a nick-name for Joseph "the 40. _____."
They plotted to 41. _____ Joseph and throw him in a cistern.
42. _____, the oldest of Joseph's brothers, told the brothers 43. _____ to kill him. He hoped to return later and 44. _____ him. He wanted to remain on everyone's 45. _____ _____, but it didn't work out for him.

v. 23-28 The brothers yanked that special 46. _____ off of Joseph. They threw him in a 47. _____.
They sat, 48. _____ a little food as Joseph lay in a pit, and they dreamed of 49. _____. His brothers were 50. _____.
Traveling salesmen passed by and 51. _____ said, "What are we going to get if we just kill Joseph? Let's get rid of him and his dreams and make some 52. _____ in the process."
Judah was an ancestor of 53. _____.
The brothers agreed and Joseph was sold for 54. ____ ounces of silver. Joseph didn't have much 55. _____ —even when they sold him.
Joseph was sold to 56. _____. Though Joseph was 57. _____ and 58. _____ off to Egypt, he was 59. _____.

v. 29-35 Rueben returned to the pit to 60. _____ Joseph and found it 61. _____.

The boys cooked up a plan to 62. _____ what had happened to Joseph. But the boys showed their 63. _____ not just to Joseph but also to their 64. _____. Jacob was 65. _____. He tore his 66. _____, put on 67. _____, and 68. _____ uncontrollably. But Jacob would not be 69. _____.

Jacob 70. _____ Joseph was dead, so he 71. _____ like he was dead. We are the same. We are set 72. _____ from sin when we accept Christ; but if we allow Satan to make us 73. _____ we are still 74. _____ and 75. _____ of sin, we 76. _____ as if those sins control us, and feel 77. _____ all the time.

v. 36 When Joseph arrived in Egypt he was 78. _____ again to Potiphar, one of Pharaoh's 79. _____. Though things looked bad, 80. _____ was at work in all that happened to Joseph. God used the sin of others to get Joseph to the exact 81. _____, at the precise 82. _____, where Joseph would be needed to save his 83. _____, all of 84. _____, and the 85. _____ of God's 86. _____."

Unit 2 God's Nation Begins
Lesson 15 God's Bumpy Road
Gen. 39-41

Essential Question: How does God work through the hard times in our lives?

v. 1 Potiphar was an Egyptian religious name meaning "devoted to the sun." He was Pharaoh's official and served as 'chief of 1. _____" or head of Pharaoh's "2. _____ _____".

v. 2-7 Going from 3. _____ _____ of a very wealthy man to a 4. _____ was harsh. But 5. _____ was with Joseph, and everything he touched 6. _____ _____.

How often do we 7. _____ to God about our 8. _____ or 9. _____ events in our life? God uses these time to teach us to 10. _____ Him, 11. _____ us, and make us 12. _____.

Joseph's 3. _____ _____, and 14. _____ proved to Potiphar that Joseph's God was 15. _____. Our actions and work habits should show our teachers and our bosses we are 16. _____ followers too.

† List 2 things you **DO** that show—without words—you are a Christian.

_____

† Imagine you are picked up in the middle of the night from your house. You are taken to Budapest where you are to live with a family and you do all the work. You get up at 5 am to prepare, work all day, and make sure they are all settled in their beds before you get to go to bed. They don't speak English. You don't speak Magyar (Hungarian).

† How do you feel? _____

Walking Law and History: Genesis/ 78

† What is the hardest part of your day? _____

† What do you have to learn? _____

† How would you get through each day? _____

_____

v. 8-10 Joseph knew he was blessed because he 17. _____ _____ before God.

Joseph made sure he was never 18. _____ with this woman. He didn't want to be 19. _____. He told her 20. "_____!" He didn't try to make 21. _____ to do wrong. He called it what it was—22. _____.

Joseph knew this sin would be found out, and he would 1.) hurt his 23. _____ of the one true God, 2.) hurt his 24. _____, and 3.) hurt his 25. _____ with God. Joseph understood if he did this wicked thing he would sin against 26. _____.

v. 11-12 Potiphar's wife did not 27. _____ _____.

Joseph didn't try to 28. _____ with her. He didn't try to 29. _____ his view again. He didn't stop and 30. _____ the matter and the wickedness of it. He 31. _____!

v. 13-18 Potiphar's decided to 32. _____ _____ with Joseph.

† How do you feel when you are accused wrongly? _____

_____

† What do you do? _____

_____

It doesn't seem as though Joseph 33. _____ himself or tried to set the record straight. In this way he was a picture of 34. _____.

v. 19-20a Potiphar 35. _____ he had to accept his wife's story. She was his wife, a woman of 36. _____, and Joseph was a 37. _____. God was with Joseph because he was only put in 38. _____.

v. 20b-23 Again we are told that the Lord was 39. _____ Joseph. We are told this 40. ____ times in this chapter alone. God caused the warden to like Joseph, and he put Joseph 41. _____ _____ of all the prison. Joseph could do anything but 42. _____.

Ch 40:1-5 The cupbearer was in charge of pharaoh's 43. _____. The baker was in charge of pharaoh's 44. _____. These two men were in 45. _____ _____, and were supposed to keep pharaoh 46. _____.

After they had been there a while, both men had a 47. _____ on the same night. Each dream was reported as having 48. _____.

v.6-7 Joseph was not wallowing in 49. _____-_____. He was not sitting around and saying, ¡God why me?¡ He noticed the 50. _____ of _____.

† Do you notice when others are not doing well? _____
_____

† Does the world revolve around you, or do you think about others? _____
_____

v. 8 Joseph knew where the real source of 51. _____ and 52. _____ came from: God.

God can speak through 53. _____, but not all dreams are from 54. _____.
The Bible also warns us that 55. _____ _____ will use dreams.

v. 9-11 The cupbearer told his dream 56. _____. It was about three vines that ripened instantly and he filled pharaoh's cup with its wine.

v. 12-15 Joseph told the man what his dream 57. _____.
Three 58. _____ = three 59. _____
60. _____ pharaoh's cup = 61. _____ from prison and being returned to his duties

Because Joseph did the cupbearer a 62. _____ by telling him the good news of his dream, Joseph asked him for a 63. _____.

v. 16-19 Joseph told him the bad news. Joseph was 64. _____ to deliver the 65. _____ _____ and the 66. _____ with equal honesty.

Three 67. _____ = three 68. _____
The 69. _____ birds were in fact eating 70. _____

v. 20-23 Yet, Joseph was 71. _____ again.

He received 72. _____ from God, and his brothers 73. _____ him into slavery.
He worked 74. _____ and behaved with 75. _____, and was thrown in 76. _____ under false charges.
He 77. _____ dreams correctly, and he was 78. _____.

Ch 41:1-7 79. _____ years passed as Joseph remained forgotten in prison. Then 80. _____ had two dreams.

v. 8-13 First thing in the morning, he went to his 81. _____ and 82. _____ _____. Yet, they could not 83. _____ these dreams. God 84. _____ the knowledge from them so 85. _____ would be remembered and lifted up.

The cupbearer 86. _____ the promise he forgot.

v.14-16 Joseph was sold at about 87. _____ Forgotten for 88. _____ years.

When we think God isn"t doing anything, He is really developing our 89. _____ and 90. _____ us into the image of 91. _____.

But Joseph gave 92. _____ all the 93. _____ and all the 94. _____.

v. 17-24 Pharaoh gave Joseph a little more 95. _____ in his retelling of the dreams.

v. 25-32 The seven good cows and good grains represented seven 96. _____ _____ for the crops. The seven ugly cows and withered grains also meant seven 97. _____. These years would be years of 98. _____ _____ or no crops.

Joseph told pharaoh since God gave him the dream 99. _____ in different forms, God was 100. _____ about these events happening, and they would happen 101. _____.

Joseph's life seemed to come in two's:
Two 102. _____ about him and his brothers

Two 103. _____

Two 104. _____ of his fellow inmates he interpreted

Two 105. _____ of pharaoh he interpreted

v. 33-36 Joseph not only gave pharaoh the 106. _____ of the dreams, he also offered a 107. _____ to help them survive what was to come.

1.) Pharaoh needed an official to 108. _____ a group of officials

2.) This group of officials was to 109. _____ no less than 1/5 of the crops for the next 7 years

3). This food was to be 110. _____ in the cities, and kept for the years of famine. Joseph understood that God had given pharaoh this information so they could plan ahead, and be saved.

Joseph was 111. _____ in his advice and showed his skill at 112. _____.

v. 37-40 Pharaoh was 113. _____ by Joseph, his 114. _____, the hand of 115. _____ on him, and the 116. _____.

v. 41-45 Like 117. _____ and the 118. _____ _____, pharaoh put Joseph in 119. _____ of everything he had, his whole kingdom. A 120. _____, a 121. _____, and a 122. _____, Joseph was now the second most 123. _____ man in all of Egypt.

Joseph was promoted to vizier at age 124. ____

Total of 125. ____ years from the 126. _____ to the 127. _____.

God is never in a 128. _____. When we are in a 129. _____ or 130. _____ situation we have to remember God is in 131. _____, and will be 132. _____ to complete the work He started in us in His time.

The 133. _____ _____ was used by the king to impress the royal seal into wax or clay as proof of a document's authenticity.

Pharaoh also dressed him in royal 134. _____, gave him private 135. _____, a 136. _____, and some expensive 137. _____.

Pharaoh also gave Joseph an Egyptian 138. _____.

Then to top off everything, Joseph was given a 139. _____.

v. 46-49 Joseph's new position not only got him out of the dark 140. _____ _____, but now he 141. _____ throughout Egypt on pharaoh's business. He ended up saving up so much food he 142. _____ _____ of how much was stored.

v. 50-52 Joseph also prospered in those seven years of plenty. He had two 143. _____. Joseph gave them 144. _____ names because he had not forgotten where he came from. 145. _____ means ïForget,î because God made him forget his trouble, and 146. _____ means ïFruitful,î because God made him fruitful in the land of his suffering.

v. 53-57 The Bible says it was a 147. _____-_____ famine. Joseph now 148. _____ the storehouses and 149. _____ grain back to the Egyptians and to foreigners in need.

Ways that Joseph was a picture of 150. _____:
1. Was a shepherd.
2. Loved by his father.
3. Sent to his brothers.
4. Hated by his brothers.
5. Prophesied his coming glory.

6. Rejected by his brothers.
7. Endured unjust punishment from his brothers.
8. Sentenced to the pit.
9. Delivered to the pit, though a leader knew he should go free.
10. Sold for pieces of silver.
11. Handed over to the Gentiles.
12. Regarded as dead, but raised out of the pit.
13. Went to Egypt.
14. Made a servant.
15. Tempted severely, but did not sin.
16. Falsely accused.
17. Made no defense.
18. Cast into prison, and numbered with sinners and criminals.
19. Endured unjust punishment from Gentiles.
20. Associated with two other criminals; one is pardoned and one is not.

Name _____

Unit 2 Homework Review #4

1. What was Jacob's pay after he earned his wives? _____
2. What did Laban accuse Jacob of when he chased him down? _____
   _____
3. Who had done the thing Jacob was accused of? _____
4. After 20 years had past, why was Jacob still afraid to return home? _____
   _____
5. What peace offering did Jacob send ahead to Esau before they met? _____
   _____
6. How did Esau welcome Jacob? _____
7. Describe the event that led up to Jacob's name being changed. _____
   _____
   _____

What was the new name? _____

8. Complete these sentences from your lesson 14 notes:

   Enoch showed the 6. _____ of faith, Noah showed the 7. _____

   of faith, Abraham showed the 8. _____ of faith, Isaac showed the

   9. _____ of faith, and Jacob showed the 10. _____ of faith.

   Along these lines we could say that Joseph showed the 11. _____ of faith.

9. Describe Joseph's dreams AND their meanings. _____
   _____

10. Describe the steps of Joseph's journey from his home to the place God needed him to be.
    _____
    _____

Unit 2 God's Nation Begins

Lesson 16 Testing and Changed Hearts
Gen. 42-44

Essential Question: What can we learn about testing from Joseph's brothers?

v. 1-5 Jacob asked his boys, ìWhy do you just keep 1. _____ at each other?î

Or was something more going on? Joseph's brothers sold him to merchants on their way to 2. _____. Were 3. _____ glances exchanged anytime anyone mentioned this neighboring land? Did the 4. _____ of Egypt remind them of the 5. _____ they had done to their brother, and so now they 6. _____ the thought of going there too, even if it meant they would die of hunger if they didn't go?

Guilt is 7. _____ and keeps us from moving 8. _____. God wants us to know we are 9. _____, and He won't act on our sins if we 10. _____ to Him.

Jacob didn't allow 11. _____ to travel with them.

v. 6-9 The boys arrived in Egypt and went to the 12. _____ in charge of selling grain to everyone.
He had an 13. _____ _____.
He was dressed in royal 14. _____ _____.
He spoke 15. _____.
And he was the second most 16. _____ man in all the land.
The brothers did not 17. _____ him. Almost 18. ____ years had past and Joseph had 19. _____ a lot.

Joseph, however, 20. _____ all of them. And when they 21. _____

before him he remembered the 22. _____ he had when he still lived at home with them.

# of Bows 23. ____

It is amazing to see how God can take the 24. _____ done to us and work out His perfect plan for our lives. To move us to where He wants for His 25. _____ and our great 26. _____.

Joseph was 27. _____ by God to deal 28. _____ with his brothers. He first accused them of being 29. _____.

v. 10-17 Joseph grilled them, saying 30. ____ times they were spies.

Joseph said he would release 31. ____ of them to return home to get their fabled brother, and the rest would wait in 32. _____ until he returned.

Joseph threw them all in 33. _____ for 34. ____ days.

v. 18-20 Joseph said that he feared 35. _____, and didn't want their 36. _____, his family, to die of starvation because he held them. He released all but 37. ____.

v. 21-24 The brothers started 38. _____ amongst themselves, as Joseph stood nearby and 39. _____. He only spoke 40. _____, and used an 41. _____.

They were so 42. _____ about what had happened 20 years ago before, they believed what they did then was a 43. _____ _____ of the 44. _____ they were going through 45. _____.

A 46. _____ _____ sees 47. _____ everywhere. We are always waiting for the 48. _____ we know we deserve for our hidden actions.

This interaction of his brothers brought Joseph to 49. _____.
His father could now be showing his 50. _____-_____ brother the same 51. _____ treatment. His brothers seemed to feel 52. _____ for what they had done to Joseph, but how did they treat 53. _____?

v. 25-28 Joseph instructed his workers to 54. _____ the _____ order and 55. _____ the money they had paid for it. They stood accused of being 56. _____, and the silver in their bags could prove them to be 57. _____. They were 58. _____ _____, and they understood 59. _____ hand in it all. They saw it as their long overdue punishment, but God was using it to 60. _____ them: both to 61. _____ and to 62. _____ them with Joseph.

v. 29-36 He believed Joseph had been 63. _____ for 20 years. Now he quickly wrote off 64. _____, and he feared over 65. _____ loss as well.

Jacob seemed to believe that 66. _____ things were 67. _____ him and God was not 68. _____ enough to work things out. Too many of us feel this way, but God is the 69. _____-_____, 70. _____ of the heavens and the earth. Nothing is 71. _____ for Him.

v. 37-38 Jacob 72. _____ to send Benjamin, leading 73. _____ to swear, on the lives of his 74. _____, he would bring Benjamin back 75. _____. If they left soon, both 76. _____ and 77. _____ could be saved. Jacob was 78. _____ in his refusal.

Ch. 43: 1-2 Simeon was left forgotten to 79. _____ _____ in prison.

Jacob and his remaining family ate all the 80. _____ they had purchased, and when they ran out, Jacob instructed them to 81. _____ for more.

v. 3-10 82. _____ reminded dad they would not even get an 83. _____ with the official who was selling the grain unless 84. _____ traveled with them.

Jacob vented his 85. _____ and 86. _____.

Judah then 87. _____ that Benjamin would return 88. _____.

v. 11-14 Jacob saw his only other 89. _____ was for him and his family to 90. _____. Thus, Jacob sent 91. _____ to soothe the official: the 92. _____ from the first purchase, and enough 93. _____ for a new purchase. He then, finally, asked 94. _____ to watch over them.

Even after his 95. _____, Jacob sounded 96. _____. Jacob didn't 97. _____ his boys to bring back his sons, and he didn't even seem to trust 98. _____ to help.

† How often do you pray but don't expect God will do anything? _____

† Will your faith move mountains? _____

v. 15-18 Seeing his brothers again, Joseph instructed the man in charge of running his home to take them to his 99. _____ and prepare a 100. _____ in their 101. _____.

The brothers didn't understand and were 102. _____ they were going to be 103. _____ and made 104. _____.

v. 19-23 They frantically tried to 105. _____ what happened on their first trip, but Joseph's steward assured them, he had 106. _____ payment for their grain the first time, so the money must have been a 107. _____ from their God.

It seems as though Joseph had shared his 108. _____, unlike 109. _____.

v. 24-30 When Joseph arrived they presented the 110. _____ to him and all 111. _____ brothers bowed down, again fulfilling the 112. _____ he had as a child.

# of Bows 113. _____

Then he asked about their father. They answered and 114. _____ again.

# of Bows 115. _____

The reunion was very 116. _____. Joseph 117. _____ him and hurried from the room so that he could 118. _____ for joy in private.

v. 31-34 Joseph pulled himself together, returned, and the 119. _____ began. Though they all ate together, and the men were all in the same room, they were 120. _____.

God was bringing His chosen people here to live for 121. ____ years as He told Abraham, but they would be 122. _____, not mixed in with the rest of the Egyptian population. These two groups would not socialize during this time. This was part of God's 123. _____ over them.

Joseph 124. _____ his brothers in the 125. _____ of their birth.

They 126. _____ while there was a 127. _____ in the land. Food could not be grown. He gave all his brothers 128. _____ to eat but Benjamin got 129. ____ times more.

Ch 44:1-5 Joseph instructed his steward to give the 11 men as much 130. _____ as they could 131. _____ and also to put their 132. _____ back into their bags. The final test was then set when Joseph gave the servant his 133. _____ ____ to put into 134. _____ sack.

v. 6-10 The steward was instructed to 135. _____ after the brothers and spring Joseph's trap. He 136. _____ them of 137. _____ Joseph's cup. The brothers 138. _____ any knowledge of the cup. They claimed their 139. _____ by reminding the man they had brought back the 140. _____ from the first purchase and more for the second. Clearly they didn't 141. _____ to steal; they had 142. _____ money to buy as much grain as they needed. They went even further and said, Ï If any of us has this cup, he's 143. _____ and the rest are your master's 144. _____ .Ó

The steward altered the terms. If the cup was found, whomever had it would become a 145. _____ of his master and the rest could return 146. _____ in 147. _____ .

v. 11-13 The steward went through the motions of searching 148. _____ _____ in the order he saw his master use.

The brothers had indeed 149. _____ . They saw Benjamin in 150. _____ but they didn't 151. _____ him. They tore their 152. _____ and

153. _____ to the official's home with Benjamin.

v. 14-17 The brothers re-entered Joseph's home and 154. _____ at his 155 _____.

# of Bows 156. ____

Joseph ramped up their 157. _____ a little more.

158. _____ spoke up for them. He 159. _____ _____ to what they had done years before. After his confession he told Joseph they were all his 160. _____, not just Benjamin. They would not 161. _____ him. They were willing to give up their lives as privileged sons of a wealthy man to pay, not for the 162. _____, but for the more serious 163. _____ from years ago.

Though 164. _____ of the sin of stealing the cup, they were 165. _____ of a far greater sin. We also see ourselves as 166. _____, but we are still 167. _____. God doesn't rank sins like we do. Sin is sin. We can't 168. _____ from 169. _____, and 170. _____ doesn't erase the 171. _____. Only the 172. _____ of Jesus can set us free.

He said he wouldn't hold the 173. _____ with the 174. _____. Only the one was required to 175. _____, the others could 176. _____.

v. 18-24 177. _____, in great humility, stepped forward and explained to Joseph how 178. _____ Benjamin was to their 179. _____.

v. 25-32 Here Judah showed they not only 180. _____ for Benjamin, but he also showed he 181. _____ _____ for his 182. _____ and did not want to bring him further pain.

Walking Law and History: Genesis/   94

v. 33-34 Now Judah made the 183. _____ _____. Seeing that the official only wanted 184. ____ man, Benjamin, he offered 185. _____ in his brother's place.

Judah was the same man who suggested 186. _____ Joseph 20 years earlier.

187. _____ offered to suffer with Israel, and 188. _____ wanted to take the place of his unsaved brothers. We show we have been 189. _____ by God through 190. _____ _____.

This chapter gives evidence of how Joseph's brothers had 191. _____.

- There was no 192. _____ of Benjamin
- They didn't 193. _____ each other for stealing the cup
- They 194. _____ _____ and went back to Egypt
- They 195. _____ themselves for the sake of Benjamin
- They knew everything happened because of their 196. _____ _____ _____
- They offered 197. _____ as slaves
- They 198. _____ about their father
- Judah offer to 199. _____ himself for his brother

God's greatest 200. _____ for us is our changed 201. _____.

† Is God waiting for you to make a change in your life? _____
† What are you going to do about it? _____
_____

Unit 2 God's Nation Begins
Lesson 17 Family Reunion
Gen. 45-46:30

Essential Question: What does God do in relationships?

Joseph 1. _____ his ten brothers, but they didn't 2. _____ him. He 3. _____ them, 4. _____ them, 5. _____ they bring back their youngest brother, and when all 11 returned, he 6. _____ with them, 7. _____ Benjamin, and put them through a tough 8. _____.

His brothers were reminded of their 9. _____ in their actions against 10. _____ years before.

But they had 11. _____.

They didn't 12. _____ Benjamin. They wouldn't 13. _____ him when he was accused of theft. Judah 14. _____ to take his place to save both 15. _____ and his 16. _____.

v. 1-3 Joseph couldn't remain 17. _____ any longer. He had waited months testing his brothers, and saw how 18. _____ they were. He 19. _____ everyone to leave him 20. _____ with the eleven Hebrews. Then he burst out in 21. _____ _____ and told them he was Joseph.

His brothers were 22. _____. They couldn't 23. _____, and they couldn't 24. _____. They knew they deserved to be 25. _____ for what they did to Joseph. He was the second most 26. _____ man in all Egypt. He could snap his fingers and order them, 27. _____, 28. _____, 29. _____, or 30. _____.

v. 4-7 "It is all right, don't 31. _____ _____ _____ over what happened. It was all part of 32. _____ plan that I come down here 33. _____ of you. Now I am in a position to 34. _____ our whole family. Please stop worrying. I don't want to 35. _____ you; I want to 36. _____ you. 37. _____ _____ _____ _____ _____ ___ _____ _____."

Joseph understood 38. _____ was in 39. _____ of all things.

v. 8-15 Joseph said again that God had 40. _____ _____, and he 41. _____ his brothers to return home 42. _____ and get his 43. _____ and their families and bring them back.

v. 16-24 Pharaoh got 44. _____, that the men Joseph had with him were his 45. _____. Pharaoh was so 46. _____, he told Joseph to load up his brothers with supplies for the trip back to Canaan and their return trip with all their family. He told Joseph to pack everyone up and 47. _____ them to Egypt. He would give them the 48. _____ of the _____ to live in, and the best to eat.

Joseph gave the 49. _____ and 50. _____ donkeys with gifts and supplies to his brothers, dressed them in new 51. _____ and sent them off.

Benjamin received 52. _____ sets of clothes and 53. _____ _____ pounds of silver. As they left, Joseph reminded them not to 54. _____ on their way home!

v. 25-28 Jacob had a little trouble 55. _____ the son he had thought dead for over 20 years was still 56. _____, and not only alive but a 57. _____ in Egypt. It sounds like he might of almost fainted. The boys' story and the many things they brought back with them 58. _____ and 59. _____ Jacob, and he was 60. _____ to go to Egypt and see his beloved son again.

Jacob wouldn't believe until he heard Joseph's 61. _____ and saw the
62. _____ he had sent. Most people will not believe in God and His Son Jesus Christ
until they 63. _____ His words and see the blessings in 64. _____ lives.

† What are you doing to share your faith with others? _____
_____

Ch 46:1-4 Israel 65. _____ and 66. _____.
God again 67. _____ directly to Jacob as he prepared to 68. _____. God
changed his name to Israel, but He called him Jacob. God told him not to be 69. _____,
to go to Egypt. But God would go 70. _____ him and make Jacob's family a
71. _____ _____.

v. 5-7 Jacob, 72. _____ continued on the journey to Egypt.
Skip verse 8-25. This is a list of all Jacob's children and their children at the time of entering Egypt.

v. 26-27 73. ____ men plus Jacob, Joseph, and his two boys already in Egypt was a total of
74. ____ men plus wives and daughters who moved into their new homes as foreigners in a
distant land. Over the next 75. _____ years, this family of 70 men and their families would grow
to a 76. _____ of more than 77. ____ _____ people.
Like many 78. _____ _____ of God, Israel had a 79. _____
beginning.

- ❖ It took Abraham 80. ____ years to add one son - Isaac
- ❖ Isaac waited 81. ____ years to add another son - Jacob
- ❖ Jacob spent 82. ____ or ____ years to add twelve sons and one daughter
- ❖ But in 83. _____ years, Israel would leave Egypt with 600,000 men
- ❖ It took this family 215 years to grow from 84. ____ to ____, but in another 430 years

they grew to 85. _____ _____.

v. 28-30 And Jacob said he could die a 86. _____ _____ because he had seen his son 87. _____ again.
Jacob also knew God had 88. _____ making Joseph his 98. _____ and 90. _____ of the family after him.

Unit 2 God's Nation Begins
Lesson 18 Foreigners in a Foreign Land
Gen. 46:31-47:31

Essential Question: Does God have a plan in all situations?

v. 31-34 Joseph, led by 1. _____, told his family he was going to tell pharaoh his family had 2. _____ and they were 3. _____. The Egyptians were 4. _____ and thought sheep and shepherds were 5. _____ and _____ in society. This would make the Egyptians want to 6. _____ _____ _____ of this new group. They had two strikes against them: they were 7. _____, and they worked with 8. _____. In this way God set Joseph's family 9. _____. This would be a pure line for the coming 10. _____.

Ch 47:1-4 He took 11. ____ of his brothers. They all answered pharaoh that they were 12. _____. They also asked for 13. _____ to live in 14. _____ for a time.

v. 5-6 Pharaoh told Joseph he could settle his family 15. _____ he liked, and Goshen was a 16. _____. He offered to 17. _____ some of the brothers to tend his own flocks.

v. 7-10 Next Joseph brought his 18. _____ in to meet pharaoh. The first thing Jacob did was to 19. _____ pharaoh.
Jacob called his life a 20. _____. Jacob understood that Egypt was not his 21. _____. Then he said he had lived only a 22. _____, 23. _____ time of 24. ____ years.
Then Jacob 25. _____ pharaoh again and left.

v. 11-12 Joseph got his family 26. _____, and made sure they all had 27. _____ to eat.

v. 13-15 As the famine continued, people took all their 28. _____ both in Egypt and in Canaan and paid Joseph for the 29. _____ he had stored up for them. At any rate, they were in the 30. _____ of the famine years and they had 31. _____ _____ of money to buy more food. They begged pharaoh, or Joseph, for more 32. _____ so they wouldn't die.

Joseph took all the money collected, both Egyptian and Canaanite, and put it in the 33. _____ _____.

v. 16-17 Joseph told the people he would sell them food for their 34. _____, so all the people sold their livestock to Joseph for food.

v. 18-22 The following 35. _____ the people are in the same 36. _____ situation. Next they offer up both their 37. _____ and 38. _____. Only the 39. _____ who were paid directly from pharaoh had enough food and kept both their 40. _____ and their 41. _____.

v. 23-26 Joseph gave them 42. _____ to plant, and said they would now continue to give pharaoh 43. _____ of all their crops.

They needed to use the 44. _____ of the seed to 45. _____, and to have seed to 46. _____ the field the next year.

The people were 47. _____. They 48. _____ at living even though they were now 49. _____.

Pharaoh now had all the 50. _____, all the 51. _____, all the 52. _____, and all his 53. _____ were his slaves.

v. 27 Jacob's family, however, under Joseph's care 54. _____ and 55. _____.

v. 28-31 Jacob lived for a total of 56. _____ years in Egypt. He called Joseph. At 57. _____ Jacob knew he was dying, and made Joseph swear a solemn promise not to 58. _____ him in Egypt but return his body to the land God 59. _____ him. Joseph swore he would return Jacob's 60. _____ to the cave where his fathers were buried.

Unit 2 God's Nation Begins
Lesson 19 Blessings and Farewells
Gen. 48 and 49:29-50

Essential Question: How does God continue His plan on earth after one of His servants joins Him in heaven?

v. 1-4 Jacob was near 1. _____, so Joseph took his two 2. _____ and went to him.

v. 5-7 Jacob told Joseph that he was in a sense 3. _____ Manasseh and Ephraim as his own 4. _____. Not grandsons, but sons; and they would be sons of as much 5. _____ as the 6. _____ and 7. _____ born to him like Rueben and Simeon actually were.

Remember the son that received the inheritance received a 8. _____ _____ of what his father had. Both of Joseph's sons were 9. _____.

From this time on there are considered to be two main groupings of the 12 tribes of Israel

1) the twelve 10. _____ tribes
2) the twelve tribes of 11. _____

The number 12. _____ is special to God. As a number, 12 is often associated with 13. _____ or administration in God's eyes.

- ❖ There are twelve 14. _____,
- ❖ twelve 15. _____,
- ❖ twelve 16. _____ of Ishmael,
- ❖ twelve 17. _____ on Moses' altar,
- ❖ twelve 18. _____ on the high priest's breastplate,
- ❖ twelve 19. _____ of showbread,
- ❖ twelve silver platters, silver bowls, and gold pans for the service of the tabernacle,
- ❖ twelve 20. _____ to search out the land,
- ❖ twelve 21. _____ stones,
- ❖ twelve 22. _____ under Solomon,

- twelve 23. _____ in Elijah's altar,
- twelve in each group of 24. _____ and 25. _____ for Israel's worship,
- twelve 26. _____ in a day (and twelve in the night),
- twelve 27. _____ in a year,
- heaven has twelve 28. _____ of twelve 29. _____,
- and twelve 30. _____ at the gates,
- the New Jerusalem has twelve 31. _____, each with the names of the twelve apostles of the Lamb,
- and the tree of life in heaven has twelve 32. _____.

v. 8-11 Jacob 33. _____ his grandsons and 34. _____ them.

v. 12-14 Manasseh as the 35. ___ _____ on Jacob's 36. _____ and Ephraim on his 37. _____, but Jacob deliberately 38. _____ his arms and gave the blessing of the first born to the 39. _____—sound familiar? "For 40. ___ consecutive generations this reversed pattern was followed:
- 41. _____ over Ishmael
- 42. _____ over Esau
- 43. _____ over Rueben (1st born of Rachel over 1st born of Leah)
- 44. _____ over Manasseh"

v. 15-16 Jacob gave the 45. _____ blessing to both boys, but it was 46. _____ that the boy under his right hand would receive a 47. _____ _____ of this blessing.
Many of Israel's 48. _____ _____ came from these 49. ___ tribes.
This is the first mention of God as a 50. _____.

v. 17-20 Joseph thought Jacob had made a 51. _____ and tried to 52. _____

Unit 2 God's Nation Begins
Lesson 19 Blessings and Farewells
Gen. 48 and 49:29-50

Essential Question: How does God continue His plan on earth after one of His servants joins Him in heaven?

v. 1-4 Jacob was near 1. _____, so Joseph took his two 2. _____ and went to him.

v. 5-7 Jacob told Joseph that he was in a sense 3. _____ Manasseh and Ephraim as his own 4. _____. Not grandsons, but sons; and they would be sons of as much 5. _____ as the 6. _____ and 7. _____ born to him like Rueben and Simeon actually were.

Remember the son that received the inheritance received a 8. _____ _____ of what his father had. Both of Joseph's sons were 9. _____.

From this time on there are considered to be two main groupings of the 12 tribes of Israel

1) the twelve 10. _____ tribes
2) the twelve tribes of 11. _____

The number 12. ____ is special to God. As a number, 12 is often associated with 13. _____ or administration in God's eyes.

- ❖ There are twelve 14. _____,
- ❖ twelve 15. _____,
- ❖ twelve 16. _____ of Ishmael,
- ❖ twelve 17. _____ on Moses' altar,
- ❖ twelve 18. _____ on the high priest's breastplate,
- ❖ twelve 19. _____ of showbread,
- ❖ twelve silver platters, silver bowls, and gold pans for the service of the tabernacle,
- ❖ twelve 20. _____ to search out the land,
- ❖ twelve 21. _____ stones,
- ❖ twelve 22. _____ under Solomon,

- twelve 23. _____ in Elijah's altar,
- twelve in each group of 24. _____ and 25. _____ for Israel's worship,
- twelve 26. _____ in a day (and twelve in the night),
- twelve 27. _____ in a year,
- heaven has twelve 28. _____ of twelve 29. _____,
- and twelve 30. _____ at the gates,
- the New Jerusalem has twelve 31. _____, each with the names of the twelve apostles of the Lamb,
- and the tree of life in heaven has twelve 32. _____.

v. 8-11 Jacob 33. _____ his grandsons and 34. _____ them.

v. 12-14 Manasseh as the 35. _____ on Jacob's 36. _____ and Ephraim on his 37. _____, but Jacob deliberately 38. _____ his arms and gave the blessing of the first born to the 39. _____ —sound familiar? "For 40. ____ consecutive generations this reversed pattern was followed:
- 41. _____ over Ishmael
- 42. _____ over Esau
- 43. _____ over Rueben (1st born of Rachel over 1st born of Leah)
- 44. _____ over Manasseh"

v. 15-16 Jacob gave the 45. _____ blessing to both boys, but it was 46. _____ that the boy under his right hand would receive a 47. _____ _____ of this blessing.
Many of Israel's 48. _____ _____ came from these 49. ____ tribes.
This is the first mention of God as a 50. _____.

v. 17-20 Joseph thought Jacob had made a 51. _____ and tried to 52. _____

Jacob's hands. But Jacob made it clear he 53. _____ exactly what he was doing.

v. 21-22 Now he passed the torch of Abraham's 54. _____ to 55. _____.
Skip ch 49:1-28 This is a list of the individual blessing to each of Jacob's sons.

v. 29-32 Jacob now told all his boys to 56. _____ him in the cave Abraham had purchased. Because of his status and his connection with Joseph he could have been buried like a 57. _____, but he wanted to be buried in a 58. _____ _____ in the middle of a second rate country. He knew where he 59. _____.

v. 33 Patriarchs are the men who are the 60. _____ of families, tribes, or the 61. _____ of a group. The patriarchs of Israel are 62. _____, 63. _____ and 64. _____.

Ch 50:1-3 Joseph instructed that his father's body be 65. _____. Yet the people of Egypt mourned for 66. ____ days. At this time Egyptians mourned for their pharaoh for 67. ____ days. Instead they mourned him 68. ____ days 69. _____.

v. 4-14 Pharaoh gave him 70. _____ and Joseph went back to Canaan along with Pharaoh's 71. _____ and 72. _____, Joseph's 73. _____ _____ and all his 74. _____. There were also 75. _____ and 76. _____.
Joseph was 77. ____ .

v. 15-18 The brothers were still living in the 78. _____. They most likely 79. _____ _____ this story, but they didn't feel they could just ask Joseph for 80. _____.
The idea that his brothers, still thought he wanted 81. _____, 82. _____ him so much he cried.
Then the brothers threw themselves at Joseph's 83. _____ and offered to be his

slaves.

# of Bows 84. _____

v. 19-21 Joseph made it clear it was God's 85. _____ to hand out 86. _____. Joseph was not 87. _____ with their doubt. He spoke 88. _____ to them and told them twice not to 89. _____. He did not 90. _____ them. Everything had been part of 91. _____ _____ to save many 92. _____. Joseph also promised to continue to 93. _____ for them and their families.

† Do you have Joseph's perspective in your life? _____

† Do you KNOW that everything that happens to you God can use for good? _____

† Do you have an example of God using bad in your life for good? _____

_____

The truth is, what happens in our lives is not the result of the actions of other 94. _____. 95. _____ controls everything that happens to us.

v. 22-26 Joseph lived another 96. ____ years in Egypt. Before he died, he told his brothers he too wanted to be 97. _____ in Canaan. He made his brothers swear an oath and then he died at 98. ____ Joseph was embalmed also and placed in a 99. _____ until the Israelites returned to the land God had promised. Genesis ends with 100. _____: the hope of God 101. _____ the people of Israel, the hope of God 102. _____ His promise, and the hope of returning to the 103. _____ _____.

Joseph's family waited for God to 104. _____ them from their time in Egypt, and later slavery.

Once in the land, they waited for God to 105. _____ the promised Messiah.

Now we wait for 106. _____ return.

Name _____

Unit 2 Homework Review #5

1. Why did Jacob send ten of his son's to Egypt? _____

2. Why didn't Joseph's brothers recognize him? _____
   _____

3. Why didn't Joseph just tell them who he was? _____

4. What did Joseph demand they bring back with them in order to get Simeon out of prison?
   _____

5. How did Joseph react when they came back? _____

6. What did he do for Benjamin while they dined together? _____
   _____

7. Why did Joseph have his silver cup put in Benjamin's sack? _____
   _____

8. What did the brothers do when Benjamin was accused of thieft and taken back to Egypt?
   _____

9. Why was it important that Judah offered to take his place? _____
   _____

10. After Jacob died, what were his sons still afraid of? _____

11. How did Joseph comfort them? _____
    _____

Gen. 12:1-2

The LORD had said to Abram, "Leave your country, your people and your father's household and go to the land I will show you. I will make you into a great nation and I will bless you; I will make your name great, and you will be a blessing."

Hebrews 11:8-9

By faith Abraham, when called to go to a place he would later receive as his inheritance, obeyed and went, even though he did not know where he was going. By faith he made his home in the promised land like a stranger in a foreign country; he lived in tents, as did Isaac and Jacob, who were heirs with him of the same promise.

Genesis 22:16-18

"I swear by myself, declares the LORD, that because you have done this and have not withheld your son, your only son, I will surely bless you and make your descendants as numerous as the stars in the sky and as the sand on the seashore. Your descendants will take possession of the cities of their enemies, and through your offspring all nations on earth will be blessed, because you have obeyed me."

Genesis 41:37-38

The plan seemed good to Pharaoh and to all his officials.So Pharaoh asked them, "Can we find anyone like this man, one in whom is the spirit of God.

Genesis 42:21-22

They said to one another, "Surely we are being punished because of our brother. We saw how distressed he was when he pleaded with us for his life, but we would not listen; that's why this distress has come upon us." Reuben replied, "Didn't I tell you not to sin against the boy? But you wouldn't listen! Now we must give an accounting for his blood."

Genesis 50:20

You intended to harm me, but God intended it for good to accomplish what is now being done, the saving of many lives.

Proverbs 22:3-5

A prudent man sees danger and takes refuge, but the simple keep going and suffer for it. Humility and the fear of the LORD bring wealth and honor and life. In the paths of the wicked lie thorns and snares, but he who guards his soul stays far from them.